T0215550

Immersive 3D Design Visualization

With Autodesk Maya and Unreal Engine 4

Abhishek Kumar

Apress®

Immersive 3D Design Visualization: With Autodesk Maya and Unreal Engine 4

Abhishek Kumar
Varanasi, Uttar Pradesh, India

ISBN-13 (pbk): 978-1-4842-6596-3   ISBN-13 (electronic): 978-1-4842-6597-0
https://doi.org/10.1007/978-1-4842-6597-0

Managing Director, Apress Media LLC: Welmoed Spahr
Acquisitions Editor: Spandana Chatterjee
Development Editor: Matthew Moodie
Coordinating Editor: Divya Modi

Cover designed by eStudioCalamar

Cover image designed by Freepik (www.freepik.com)

Distributed to the book trade worldwide by Springer Science+Business Media New York, 1 New York Plaza, Suite 4600, New York, NY 10004-1562, USA. Phone 1-800-SPRINGER, fax (201) 348-4505, e-mail orders-ny@springer-sbm.com, or visit www.springeronline.com. Apress Media, LLC is a California LLC and the sole member (owner) is Springer Science + Business Media Finance Inc (SSBM Finance Inc). SSBM Finance Inc is a **Delaware** corporation.

For information on translations, please e-mail booktranslations@springernature.com; for reprint, paperback, or audio rights, please e-mail bookpermissions@springernature.com.

Apress titles may be purchased in bulk for academic, corporate, or promotional use. eBook versions and licenses are also available for most titles. For more information, reference our Print and eBook Bulk Sales web page at http://www.apress.com/bulk-sales.

Any source code or other supplementary material referenced by the author in this book is available to readers on GitHub via the book's product page, located at www.apress.com/978-1-4842-6596-3. For more detailed information, please visit http://www.apress.com/source-code.

Printed on acid-free paper

To mom, Usha Sinha, dad, Prof. B. K. Prasad,
and my beloved wife, Alka, for 11 fantastic years of marriage
and many more to come. To my daughter, Rishika Ryan,
and my son, Shivay Singh Ryan. I love you all.

Table of Contents

TABLE OF CONTENTS

About the Author

Dr. Abhishek Kumar awarded PhD, Doctorate in Computer Application (Research Area: Stereoscopy, 3D Animation, Design, Computer Graphics & HCI); under the supervision of professor Dr. Achintya Singhal, Associate professor, Department of computer Science, Banaras Hindu University & Master Degree in Animation & Visual Effects and in Computer Science and Bachelor of Science in Multimedia.

He is an Apple Certified Associate, Adobe Education Trainer, and is certified by Autodesk. He has trained more than 90,000 students across the globe from the field of Computer Graphics, Design & Game Technology.

Dr. Abhishek Kumar has published more than 40 research papers in international reputed SCOPUS, SCI indexed Journals and has authored several books. He holds eight patents, and his research collaborators are from the worlds' top universities.

He is an active member of the American Association for the Advancement of Science (AAAS), the Association for Computing Machinery (ACM), and the Society for Animation Studies, Singapore.

About the Technical Reviewer

 **Simon Peter Hanson** is a Canadian-born, England-based technical reviewer. With two years of experience in game and mobile application development, he specializes in mobile augmented reality. His software proficiencies include Photoshop, Maya, Unreal Engine 4, and JavaScript.

He has a BSc in psychology from the University of the West of England, Bristol, and an MSc in creative technologies from Nottingham Trent University.

Simon's current projects include an integrated mobile application for use with board games, utilizing augmented reality to add to the immersive experience of players, and creating professionally crafted custom content for Dungeons and Dragons 5th Edition. Simon is an avid electric guitar player. He lives in Nottingham, England, and he is working to make his dream of having his own development brand a reality.

Acknowledgments

It gives me immense pleasure to express my deep gratitude to my mentor, Prof. Saket Kushwaha, and Prof. Alok Kumar Rai. They are the inspiration for this endeavor.

A special Thanks you to my PhD supervisor, Dr. Achintya Singhal, an associate professor at Banaras Hindu University; without his encouragement, support, and guidance, this book would not have been possible.

I would also like to thank Simon Peter Hanson, Spandana Chatterjee, Divya Modi, and Matthew Moodie for the initiation to publish this book. Their helpful comments and suggestions resulted in numerous refinements and corrections that improved its quality.

A special thanks to Dr. Vijayakumar Varadarajan, professor at the University of New South Wales, Australia, Dr. Kalyana C. Veluvolu, professor at Kyungpook National University, South Korea, and Dr. Thinagaran Perumal, Associate Professor at Universiti Putra Malaysia for providing unconditional support.

CHAPTER 1

Design for Creative and Immersive Technology

Welcome to a journey on design for creative and immersive technology. This book goes through creating assets for visualization in Maya, texturing in Substance Painter, setting up a scene in Unreal Engine 4 (UE4), creating materials, and the final render of a scene.

This book is geared toward beginners and amateurs who have very basic knowledge of 3D tools and want to know more about advanced topics. We go through every step of the asset creation pipeline, including modeling, unwrapping, and importing.

In the end, you create a simple architectural scene that you can use as a portfolio. The goal is to show off the assets that you created.

AR, VR, and Emerging Technologies

Augmented reality (AR) and virtual reality (VR) have become very popular with the surge of highly affordable GPUs and applications harnessing the power and immersiveness of these technologies. AR and VR have applications in medical science, military simulations, education, architectural visualization, and gaming. AR and VR are two different types of technologies. Augmented reality projects digital elements into the real world by using devices like smartphones. Virtual reality is a completely immersive experience that uses VR headsets to completely surround the users within a digital world. A visual example is shown in Figure 1-1.

© Abhishek Kumar 2021
A. Kumar, *Immersive 3D Design Visualization*, https://doi.org/10.1007/978-1-4842-6597-0_1

Figure 1-1. *A visual representation of immersive technology (Source: https://*
pixabay.com/)

VR for Entertainment

VR is not limited to videogames but is making its way into other fields in our daily
lives. The pace and application may be limited for now, but there is no denying that VR
will soon be a very practical and useful gadget—used in virtual tours and education.
Figure 1-2 is a visual example of how digital elements make their way into entertainment.

Figure 1-2. *Representation of VR integration for entertainment (Source: https://*
pixabay.com/)

VR for Digital Architecture

As technology quickly advances, there are opportunities for companies to harness its potential. Many companies are investing in the development of VR applications and devices. This ranges from advertising to new ways of experiencing daily activities like shopping. VR transports people into a digital world, as represented in Figure 1-3.

Figure 1-3. *VR immerses people in the digital world (Source:* `https://pixabay.com/`*)*

It allows users to explore a house before it is built or a big theme park before visiting. It has lots of potential benefits. Visualizing a house before it is constructed is a massive benefit for the buyer. It gives the customer a good idea of what they are buying, enabling them to decide what they want to have added or removed during the planning stage before the designers and builders construct the house. This is especially useful in constructing large homes where there is a lot of work involved, and there is huge room for improvement. Figure 1-4 represents a digital construction of historical architecture.

Figure 1-4. *Digital reconstruction of historical architecture (Source:* https:// pixabay.com/)

VR for Simulation and Training

VR has other useful functions, like in military simulations and training soldiers for different combat scenarios and in aviation training, to provide immersive flight simulation experiences. You can understand why aspiring CGI programmers must do a lot of research in AR and VR technology. It not only opens doors to careers but keeps you updated on the latest developments in technology.

The military uses VR for training soldiers in situations that cannot be easily constructed using traditional methods. By using immersive technology, the military can efficiently train soldiers to deal with various kinds of situations on the battlefield. Combat scenarios with realistic explosions and weapon simulation can create an amount of stress similar to a real encounter, which is beneficial in preparing for a real-life combat scenario. Figure 1-5 shows a military simulation.

Figure 1-5. *Representation of military simulation training (Source: https://
pixabay.com/)*

VR for Product Visualization

Businesses are increasingly investing in developing tools, applications, and devices
for VR and AR support. Even though few people use it now, people become interested
in products if presented in a fancy way. It shows that a company is progressive and
interested in the quality of its products and modernization. Companies can attractively
display their product lineup.

This can attract a potential customer who may have previously overlooked the
product, which is especially useful in the automobile industry since users need to see
what kind of vehicle they are purchasing. A potential customer can virtually preview
the car they are interested in purchasing to help make their decision. A customer can
digitally explore a catalog of vehicles from the comfort of their home, and then they can
easily choose the one they like. Figure 1-6 represents the digital construction of a vehicle.

Figure 1-6. *Product visualization (Source: https://pixabay.com/)*

VR for Space Exploration Simulation

Virtual reality has found a lot of use in space and planetary exploration. It is used by scientists to train pilots to drive rovers on other planets by simulating the experience of piloting a spacecraft or rover, which are difficult to drive, and one mistake can have a high cost. Space-faring organizations must train their pilots well. Figure 1-7 represents space exploration simulation.

Figure 1-7. *Representation of space exploration simulation (Source: https://pixabay.com/)*

With all of this in mind, let's jump to the next chapter, which discusses the tools of the trade—that is, the software that we use throughout the book to create a design visualization product and an immersive 3D scene.

Tools for Architectural Visualization

Welcome to Chapter 2. This chapter introduces the software and tools used throughout the book so that you can familiarize yourself with them. These tools are not the only software that you can use, however. The skills you learn are transferrable to any DCC (digital content creation) application, whether free or paid. For example, you can easily apply the same principles used in Blender or 3DS Max for modelling, Quixel Mixer for texturing, or Unity3D as a game engine to similar software.

Maya for Design Visualization

Maya is an industry-standard modelling and content-creation software application that is used across a wide variety of fields. Experience with Maya is desirable if you want a job in the modelling, unwrapping, or animation sectors of CGI or the game industry. Initially developed by Wavefront Technologies, version 1.0 was released in February 1998. Autodesk acquired it in 2005.

In this book, we use Maya for modelling and unwrapping. Maya has robust modelling tools that simplify your work with shortcuts and accessible pie menus.

Figure 2-1 shows the default Maya interface.

© Abhishek Kumar 2021
A. Kumar, *Immersive 3D Design Visualization*, https://doi.org/10.1007/978-1-4842-6597-0_2

Figure 2-1. *The default Maya interface*

Substance Painter for PBR Texturing

Substance Painter is a 3D, physically based rendering (PBR) texturing software with a
real-time viewport. Texturing assets in Substance Painter is straightforward. Painting
in 3D and immediately seeing the effects in real time is handy, but that's not all that
makes Substance Painter so good; it is the incredible arsenal of procedural effects, smart
materials, smart masks, and generators. Figure 2-2 shows Substance Painter's default
interface when launched.

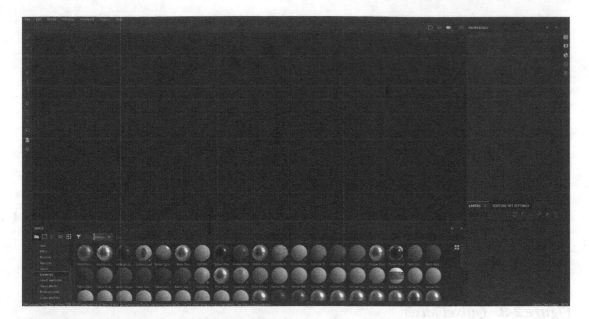

Figure 2-2. *Substance Painter interface*

The large selection of expertly crafted materials that come with a Substance suite subscription in the form of Substance Source is an excellent resource for any project. Also, Substance Share is a platform on which the Substance community shares their creations for free, which further makes Substance Painter such a good 3D texturing tool.

Quixel Mixer

Quixel Mixer is a free 3D texturing and material authoring tool for texturing assets or generating new material by leveraging Quixel Megascans, a vast library at your disposal while you are texturing. Figure 2-3 shows the Quixel Mixer interface.

Figure 2-3. *Quixel Mixer*

Acquiring Materials from Quixel Megascans

Quixel Megascans is a premium photoscanned library of assets like materials, textures, decals, grunges, imperfection maps, 3D assets, and more. It is a high-quality library used by large AAA companies for developing games and movies. It is a good resource for materials and textures that are not only realistic but also perfectly tileable and game ready. This allows you to easily create modular designs with very little effort—enabling you to be as creative as you want. It also has outstanding 3D assets, such as models and foliage that allow you to populate your scenes with realistic assets in a single click.

Quixel Megascans provides ready-to-use assets that are easily imported into any DCC tool. The best thing about Quixel Megascans is that it is completely free to use with Unreal Engine 4. Figure 2-4 shows the default Quixel Bridge interface.

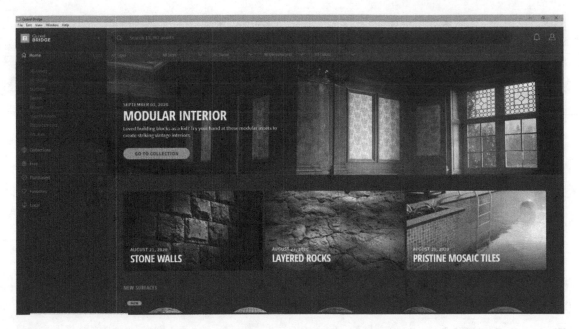

Figure 2-4. *Quixel Bridge*

Immersive Design Visualization Using UE4

Now let's look at the final software—the game engine. We are using Unreal Engine 4, which is a very popular in indie studios and many AAA studios. UE4 is very easy to use and comes with many templates and tools to help you speed up your workflow. Figure 2-5 shows the default interface for UE4's First-Person Shooter template.

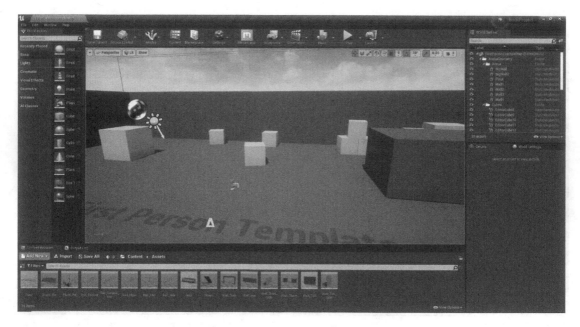

Figure 2-5. *UE4 first-person template*

Alternative Applications for Design

Blender

Blender is a free DCC application that creates models, UVs, textures, animations, visual effects (VFX), and more. This tool is a good entry point for beginners because it has no entry fee. Blender has a large community and good beginner guides on YouTube. The newer versions of Blender are easy to use, and it has a very user-friendly minimalist interface. Blender may not be popular in the AAA industry, but indie studios use it a lot because it is completely free and open source. Figure 2-6 shows Blender's default interface.

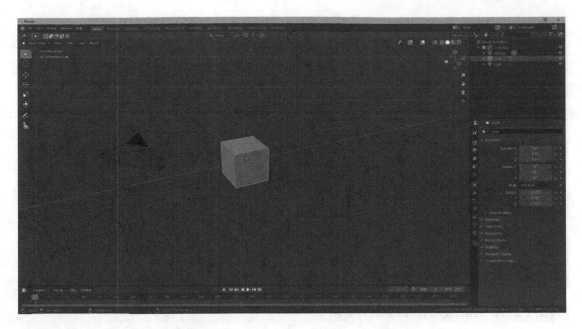

Figure 2-6. *Blender interface*

3DS Max

3DS Max is a DCC app by Autodesk. It is similar to Maya in form and function, but when it comes to layout and the method of working, it is quite different. It has slightly different controls and other hotkeys for functions. Like Maya, 3DS Max is popular in gaming studios and is widely used for making architectural assets. Figure 2-7 shows the 3DS Max interface.

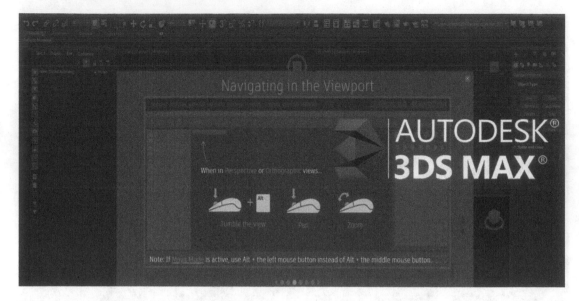

Figure 2-7. *The 3DS Max interface*

Unity3D

Unity3D is a free game engine and an alternative to Unreal Engine 4. Unity3D is very easy to use and thus is very popular among indie and smaller game studios. Unity3D is a very lightweight engine and is commonly used for creating mobile games. It is widely used by indie studios to make minimalistic platformer, arcade, and similar types of games. But that doesn't mean Unity3D can't make impressive games with good graphics. Many studios take advantage of Unity3D's simplicity and amazing graphics to create fantastic-looking games. Figure 2-8 shows the Unity3D interface.

Figure 2-8. *Unity3D*

The software that you choose is entirely your decision. The methods shown in this book are not software specific. The same techniques can be easily carried over to other tools. The more software that you are familiar with, the stronger your portfolio because it shows the flexibility of your skills. The more you know, the better.

There are certain things you need to be wary about, though.

This chapter provided a brief introduction to the software that we are using throughout the book. In the next chapter, we jump into Maya and start modelling our first asset.

CHAPTER 3

Basic of 3D Modeling: Assets

Let's start with the basics of Maya. It is important to have a good grasp of modeling before you move on to making advanced stuff. Maya is a very complex software application, and you need to memorize many hotkeys and shortcuts if you want maximum efficiency while working. After that, I cover how to block out assets and scenes in Maya.

Basic Maya Controls

Let's start with basic navigation controls. Press Alt+Left-click to rotate your viewport. Press Alt+Middle-click to pan your view. Press Alt+Right-click and drag to zoom in or out. Alternatively, you can use the scroll wheel to zoom in and out. You begin in Perspective view. You can change the view mode by pressing and holding the spacebar to open the Hotbox menu (see Figure 3-1). It is a condensed menu of all the Maya tools and tabs.

© Abhishek Kumar 2021
A. Kumar, *Immersive 3D Design Visualization*, https://doi.org/10.1007/978-1-4842-6597-0_3

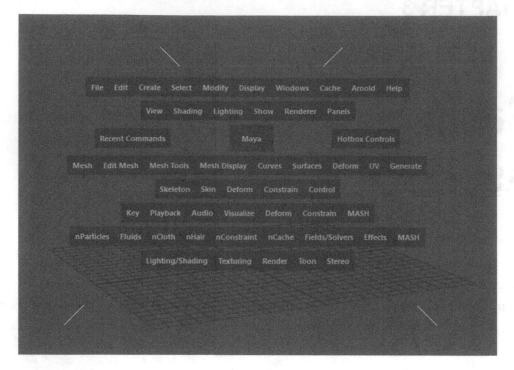

Figure 3-1. *Hotbox menu*

You can use the Hotbox menu to switch between different views. To switch views, press and hold the spacebar. Left-click while hovering over the Maya option. A pie menu shows you all the available view modes (see Figure 3-2).

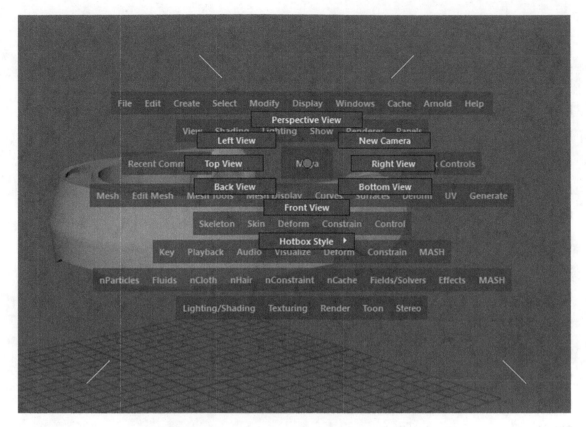

Figure 3-2. *View pie menu*

From the pie menu, you can select which view you want to switch to. By default, you work in Perspective view, but you can easily switch to another view.

Next, let's look at working with objects. Click the Poly Modeling tab (see Figure 3-3) to see all the standard primitives that you can add to your viewport.

Figure 3-3. *Poly Modeling tab*

You begin in Object mode by default. Table 3-1 lists and describes the shortcuts that you can use in Object mode.

Table 3-1. *Hotkeys and Shortcuts*

Hotkey	Function
W	Move
E	Rotate
R	Scale
Ctrl+Shift+A	Select all
Del	Delete selected objects/faces/vertices (depending on selection)
Backspace	Delete edges
Ctrl+Backspace	Delete Edges as well as vertices
Shift+D	Duplicate
Left-click	Select
Shift+Ctrl+Left-click	Add to selection
Ctrl+Left-click	Remove from selection
Ctrl+S	Save file
Ctrl+Z	Undo
Ctrl+Y	Redo
Spacebar	Toggle Minimize/Maximize editor area

There are many objects that you can add to a scene. Click the cube icon (highlighted in Figure 3-3) to add a cube to your scene.

Right-click to open the object pie menu (scc Figurc 3-4). You can use it to go to an object's edit mode to select and edit its primitives, such as vertices, edges, and faces. Select the primitives in the standard shapes that come with Maya (like sphere or cylinder), and use Figure 3-4 as a reference. An *edge* is a line on the mesh. A *vertex* is a pole where the edges intersect with one another. A *face* is an area enclosed by the edges.

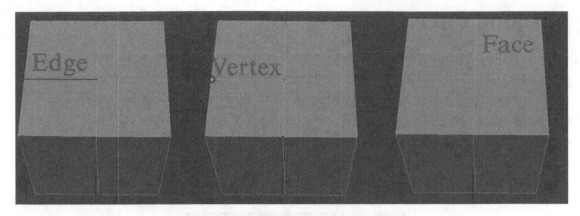

Figure 3-4. *The vertex, edge, and face primitives*

There are certain shortcut keys in edit mode that open menus that offer various functionalities and tools.

- Right-clicking presents the mode menu that allows you to switch the edit mode.

- Shift+Right-click opens a tools menu that gives access to tools like Insert Edge Loop, Multi-Cut, Merge, Bevel, and Bridge. (These tools are discussed later in the book.)

- Ctrl+Shift+Right-click opens the selected transform tool's context menu. (The transform tools are move, rotate, and scale).

- If you select an edge loop, you can slide it in any direction. Press Shift+Ctrl and use manipulators to slide the selected edge/edges.

- Select an edge or vertex and press the Shift key for the option to extrude the selected edge/face in the direction of your choice.

I could discuss more, but it is better to learn new shortcuts and techniques as you work. But before going ahead, make sure that you have practiced all the shortcuts and hotkeys discussed.

Now let's start by creating a simple headset.

Blocking Out an Asset

Let's start blocking out our assets. Blocking out is an important part of deciding what an asset looks like. A blockout gives you the freedom and flexibility to experiment with your ideas and decide what you like and what you don't. Since a blockout has very simple geometry, it can be easily modified to see what works and what doesn't.

First, let's create a cylinder by clicking the cylinder icon under the Poly Modeling tab. You need to make sure that it has many sides. You can set the parameters of your primitives in the Channel box (shortcut Ctrl+A) (see Figure 3-5).

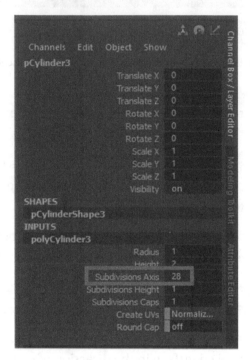

Figure 3-5. *Changing parameters*

The Channel box provides the basic parameters of your 3D model, which you can edit to make general modifications. There are Translate, Rotate, and Scale options for each axis.

Let's add 28 subdivisions to our cylinder. This makes it smoother and gives it lots of edges to work with. Now let's scale down the Y axis by pressing the R key and using a manipulator to flatten the cylinder to a value of about 0.2, as shown in Figure 3-6.

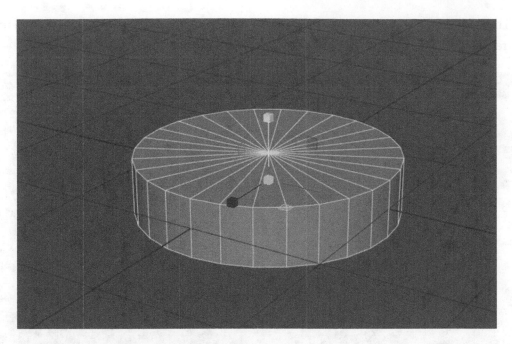

Figure 3-6. *Flattening an object*

Next, scale the cylinder along the Z-X Plane using the green square in the Scale manipulator. Make it wide— such as 7—on both the X and Z axes (see Figure 3-7).

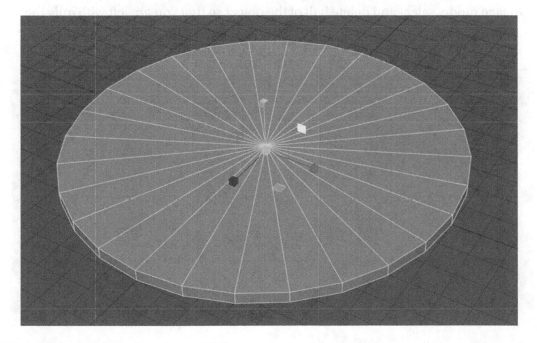

Figure 3-7. *Scaling the object wider*

Then select the top cap and bottom cap in face mode and delete them, as shown in Figure 3-8.

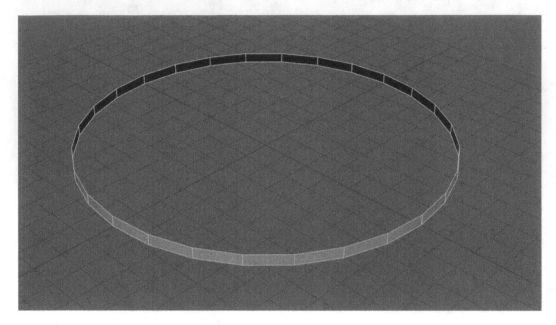

Figure 3-8. *Deleting cylinder caps*

In face mode, select and delete half of the object so that you are left with only the remaining half (see Figure 3-9).

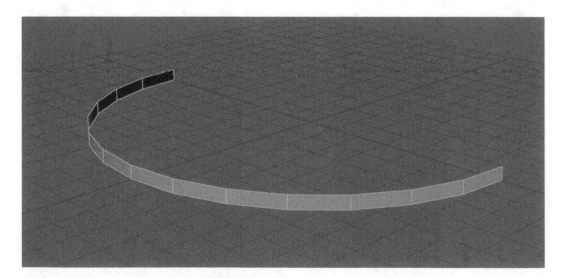

Figure 3-9. *Deleting half of the object*

Select the last two edges of the shape and make sure the Move manipulator is active. Press W if it's not. Then press the Shift key while hovering over one of the manipulators. You should see the word Extrude appear, which means if you translate the selected edges using the manipulator, it extrudes the edges. Using the Extrude feature, extrude the edges backward, as shown in Figure 3-10.

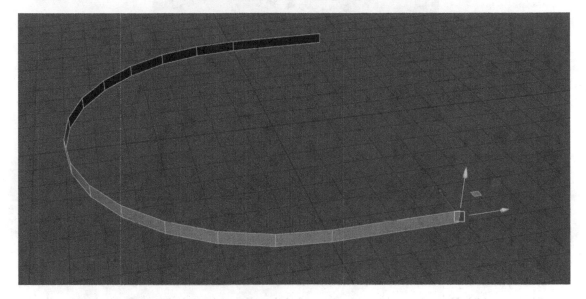

Figure 3-10. *Extruding edges backward*

Extrude can create unwanted geometry if you are not careful or if you used extrude several times on a single primitive. Select any edge and move it around to see if any unwanted faces appear. If you find extra faces that seem to overlap with the ones that you want, you should delete them by selecting the unwanted geometry and pressing the Backspace key to delete it.

Adding Symmetry

Now let's enable Symmetry on our object. Symmetry is a great tool because as you work on one side of the mesh, it copies your actions to the other side. You don't have to manually work on both sides of the mesh. To enable Symmetry, right-click and select Object mode from the pie menu. Then press Ctrl+Shift+Right-click to open the Tool menu. Symmetry is the top option (see Figure 3-11).

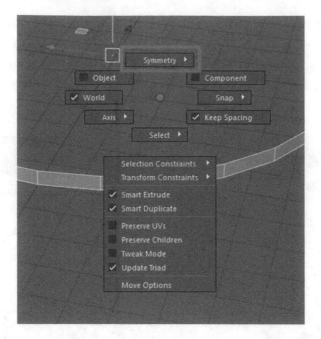

Figure 3-11. Symmetry option

Hover over Symmetry to reveal more options.

The Symmetry option has a check box next to it. By default, it is unchecked (see Figure 3-12). Hover over it, select it, and right-click to toggle it on. The same method toggles it off.

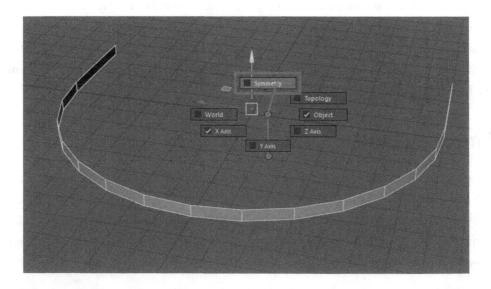

Figure 3-12. Toggling symmetry On

Once enabled, you can start editing the model. You see that any edits that you do on one side of the mesh are automatically carried over to the other side of it.

Go to the Edge Edit mode and select all the top edges. Move them up slightly and then move them back slightly, as shown in Figure 3-13.

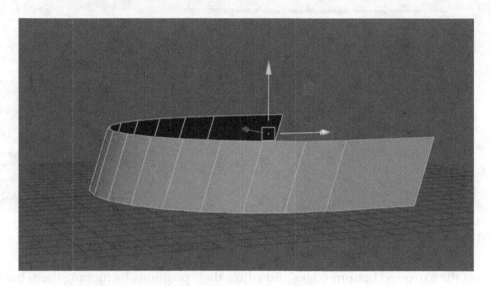

Figure 3-13. *Positioning the top edge*

Select all the bottom edges except for the last one, and extrude them downward, as shown in Figure 3-14.

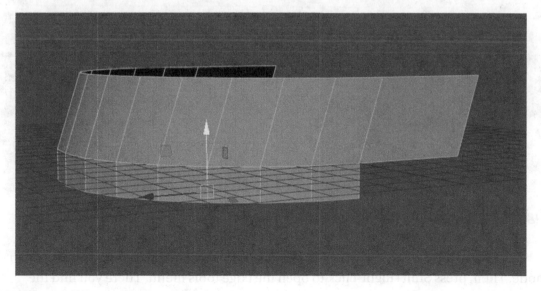

Figure 3-14. *Extruding edges down*

Select the end edges again and extrude them back once more, as shown in Figure 3-15.

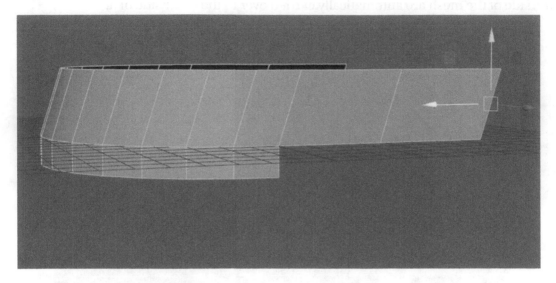

Figure 3-15. *Extrude edge back*

Select the extruded bottom edges and adjust their positions by moving them back slightly and moving them down a bit, as shown in Figure 3-16.

Figure 3-16. *Positioning our edges*

Next, let's add another edge loop to our shape. First, ensure that you are in Edge Edit mode. Then, press Shift+Right-click to open the edge tools menu. There you find the Insert Edge Loop Tool option (see Figure 3-17).

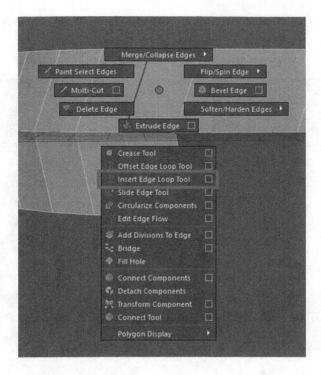

Figure 3-17. *Insert Edge Loop Tool*

Hover over it and right-click to activate the tool. Your cursor changes shape, ensuring tool activation. Now click the vertical edges to add an edge horizontally, as shown in Figure 3-18. If you click the horizontal edges, an edge is added vertically. This is best understood by doing. Try adding an edge to your mesh.

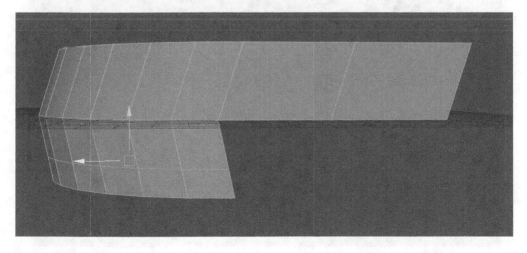

Figure 3-18. *Adding edge loop*

After that, select the bottom end edge and extrude the edge backward, as shown in Figure 3-19.

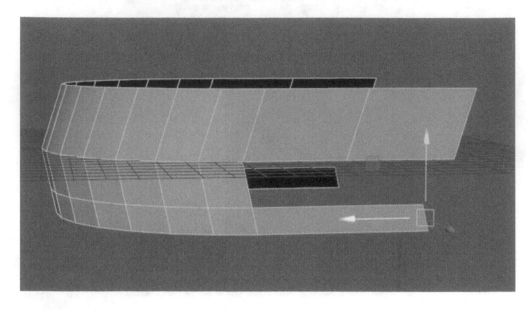

Figure 3-19. *Extruding edge back*

Select the bottom two edges at the very front of the mesh. Then press Shift+Ctrl and slide the edges up, as shown in Figure 3-20.

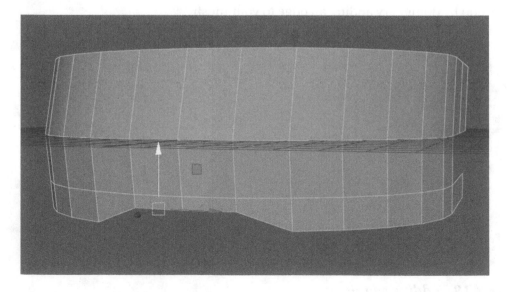

Figure 3-20. *Slide these edges up*

The edges on the mesh currently look hard and jagged. Select all the edges on the mesh by drawing a selection box around it. Make sure to select every single edge. Shift+Right-click and from the menu, select the Soften/Harden Edges option (see Figure 3-21).

Mesh normals are perpendicular lines that can be drawn facing out from each face of a mesh. They dictate how your models look. They can be hardened, softened, or flipped. After smoothing the mesh normals, the shading values are averaged, which produces a smoother look. Mesh normals can sometimes face the wrong direction, giving making your mesh look black. These are the things that you should look out for.

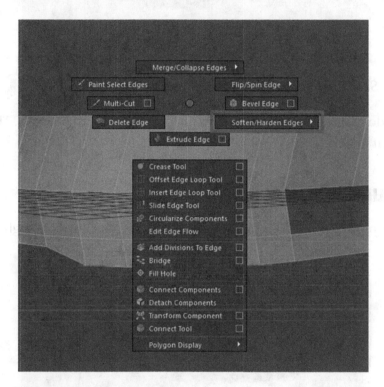

Figure 3-21. *Select Soften/Harden Edges*

Hover over Soften/Harden Edges to open a new submenu, which offers more options related to softening and hardening edges. Select the Soften Edge option and release right-click (see Figure 3-22).

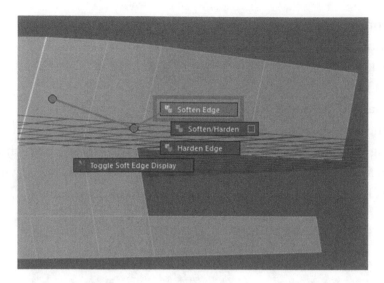

Figure 3-22. *Select Soften Edge*

Once you do that, you see that the edges no longer have hard normals. This is exactly how you want it to be.

Adding Duplicate Faces

Let's add a few more pieces to our mesh. Select and duplicate the faces highlighted in Figure 3-23.

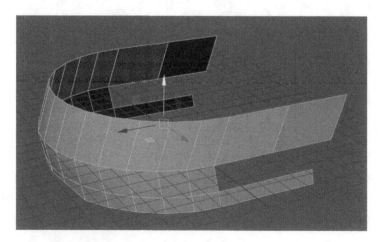

Figure 3-23. *Select these faces*

Next, press Shift+Right-click and select Duplicate Face from the list (Figure 3-24).

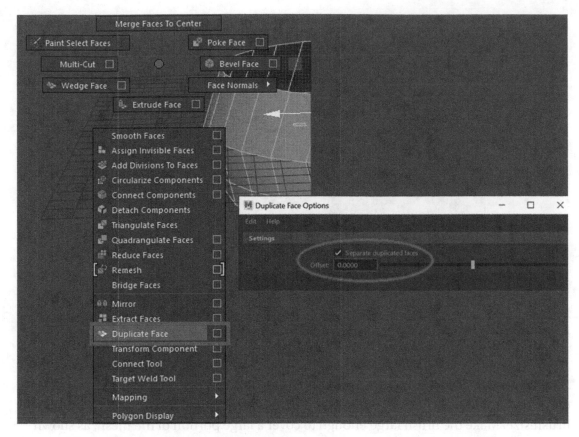

Figure 3-24. *Duplicate Face option*

Once your faces have been duplicated, they form a new object. You can also use the offset value to create space between the old and new duplicated faces. You can use the Move tool to maintain the spacing between them.

Switch to Object mode and select the mesh created by the duplicated faces. Then move them back and position them as shown in Figure 3-25. Alternatively, you can use the Channel box and enter a value of 2.0 for the X axis to translate it. If your mesh goes in the wrong direction, it means your mesh is rotated on a different axis. In that case, press Ctrl+Z to undo and enter a value of 2.0 for the Z axis (Note: Maya uses the Y axis as Up, so enter 2.0 for the Z axis).

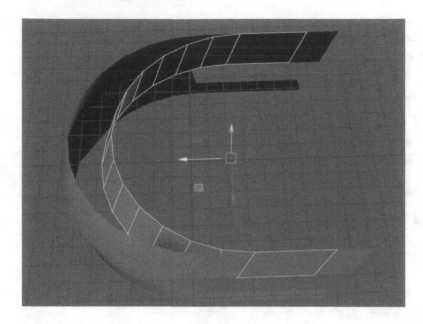

Figure 3-25. *Positioning our duplicated faces*

Now switch to the object's vertex editing mode and select the last four vertices. Press B to toggle Soft Selection on. (You can press B any time to toggle Soft Selection on or off). Press B+Middle-click and drag the mouse to the right to increase the Soft Selection brush size. Make the brush large enough to cover a large portion of the mesh, as shown in Figure 3-26.

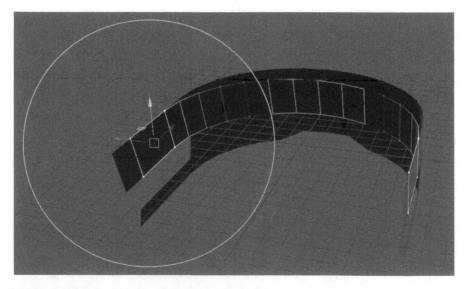

Figure 3-26. *Make Soft Selection brush large*

Then use the Move tool to position the selected vertices as shown in Figure 3-27.

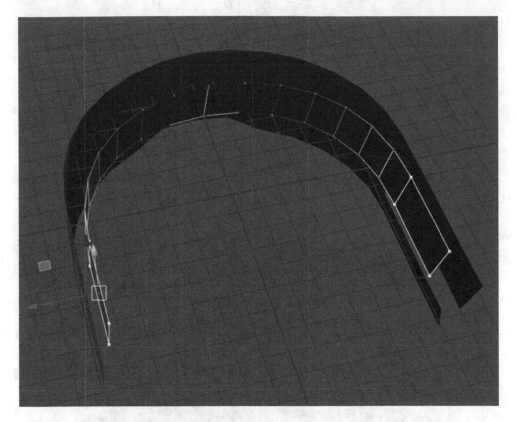

Figure 3-27. *Positioning the vertices*

If the symmetry does not work correctly on your X axis, try switching to a different Symmetry axis. To do this, go to Object mode. Press Ctrl+Shift+Right-click, go to Symmetry, and select the Z axis. This should fix your problem. Also, make sure that your mesh is centered on the grid.

Press B again to disable Soft Selection. Select and move everything so that every mesh is sitting on top of the grid, as shown in Figure 3-28. The grid overlapping the mesh is very distracting.

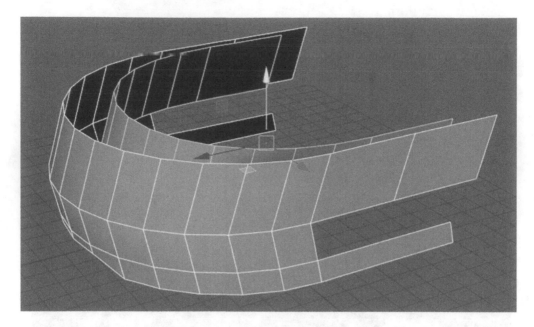

Figure 3-28. *Moving our meshes on top of the grid*

Next, go to edit mode of the smaller piece and select the edges shown in Figure 3-29.

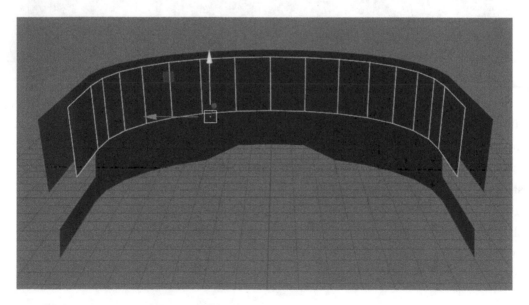

Figure 3-29. *Select the following edges*

Once selected, extrude them downward by pressing and holding the Shift key and using the Move tool, as shown in Figure 3-30.

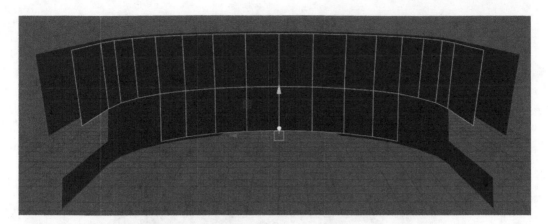

Figure 3-30. *Extrude the edges*

Note   If the extrude does not behave as intended, then disable Symmetry
and then try extruding again. Make sure that you enable Symmetry again after
extruding.

After extruding, move the edges back very slightly. There is no need to be too precise;
just make sure that the proportions look somewhat correct.

Now let's add some details to the front body of the headset. Start by adding a
couple of edge loops to the mesh. Go to Edge Select mode of the front piece and press
Shift+Right-click. From the menu, select Insert Edge Loop Tool (see Figure 3-31).

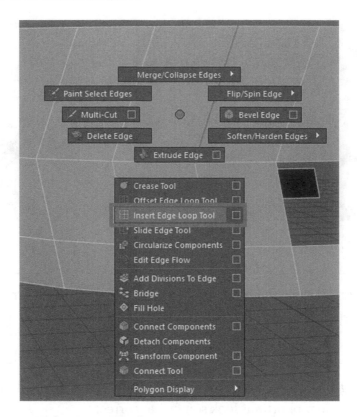

Figure 3-31. *Insert Edge Loop Tool*

Now add two edge loops, as shown in Figure 3-32.

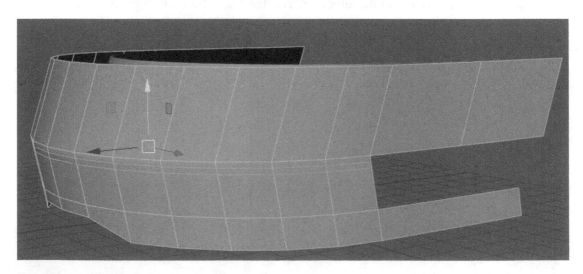

Figure 3-32. *Adding edge loops*

Select the first edge loop from the top of the shape by double-clicking it and moving it slightly forward to give it a slight curve (see Figure 3-33).

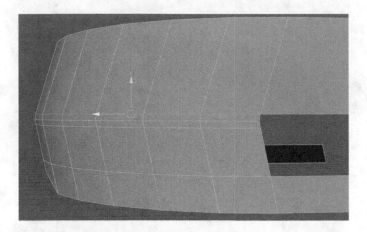

Figure 3-33. *Giving curve to our shape*

Switch to face mode and select all the faces of the mesh. You can double-click any face to select all the faces on the mesh. Shift+Right-click and select Extrude Face from the menu (see Figure 3-34).

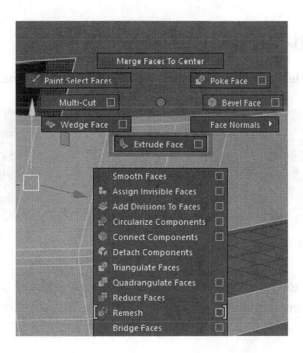

Figure 3-34. *Extrude Face*

Set the Thickness value to 0.3, as shown in Figure 3-35.

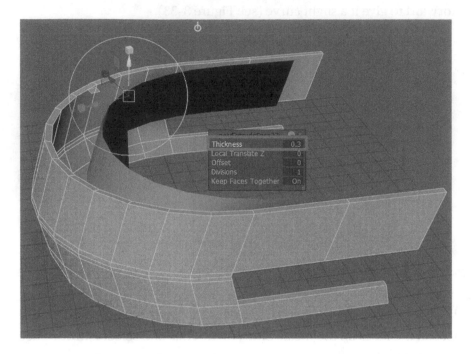

Figure 3-35. *Extruding our shape*

Using the Multi-Cut Tool

Now switch to vertex edit mode and select the Multi-Cut tool in the toolbar (see Figure 3-36).

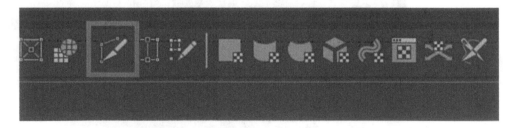

Figure 3-36. *Multi-Cut tool*

Use the Multi-Cut tool to make two edge cuts, as shown in Figure 3-37. You can press Enter to confirm the cut operation. Keep the tool active so that you can immediately perform another cut operation.

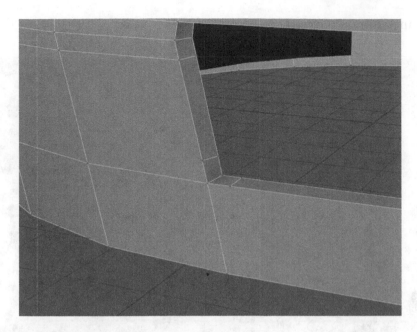

Figure 3-37. *Adding Edge-Cuts*

Adjust the vertices of the cut to make them more horizontal. It does not have to be perfect; just eyeball it. Use the Scale tool if you want to be precise. Scale downward until the vertices are aligned.

Use the Multi-Cut tool to connect the edges exactly as shown in Figure 3-38.

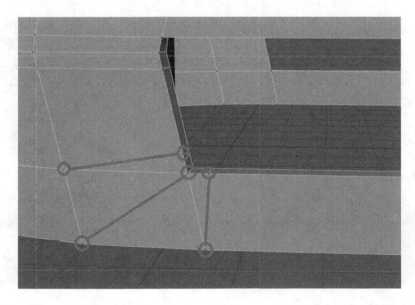

Figure 3-38. *Connect the edges*

Your connection should now look similar to Figure 3-39.

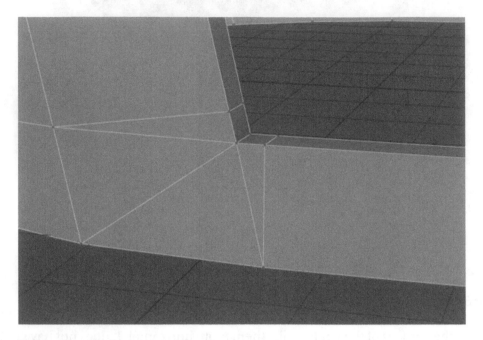

Figure 3-39. *Final edge connections*

Do the same thing on the other side of the mesh. Next, select the highlighted edges and delete them (see Figure 3-40).

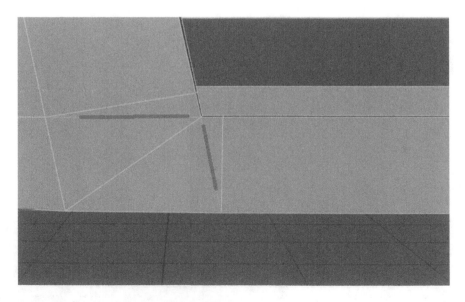

Figure 3-40. *Select and delete these edges*

Your new connection should look similar to Figure 3-41.

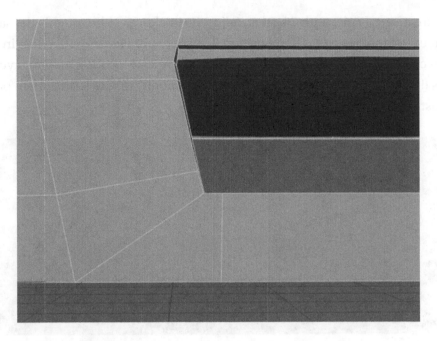

Figure 3-41. *Final connection*

Now slightly move the central edge to give it a curved, smoother look (see Figure 3-42 for reference).

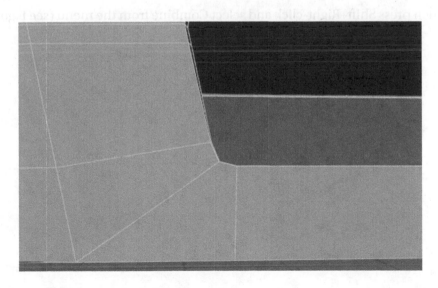

Figure 3-42. *Giving a curved shape to edges*

Joining Objects

Let's now create a cylinder with 20 sides. Adjust its thickness to be roughly the same as the front piece of the headset. Then position it as shown in Figure 3-43. While in Object mode, you can use the Channel box to enter a more precise location for your cylinder. This helps fine-tune the location if positioning it manually makes it difficult to perform small adjustments.

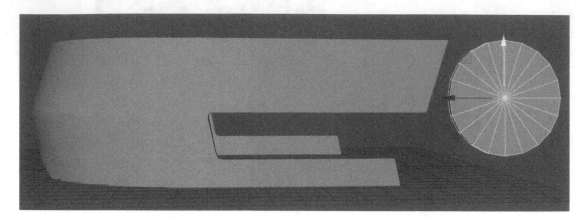

Figure 3-43.   *Positioning the cylinder*

Let's join this cylinder to the main body so that you can connect the faces and make one unified object. To begin, select the front headpiece. Shift+Left-click the cylinder to select it. Then press Shift+Right-click and select Combine from the menu (see Figure 3-44).

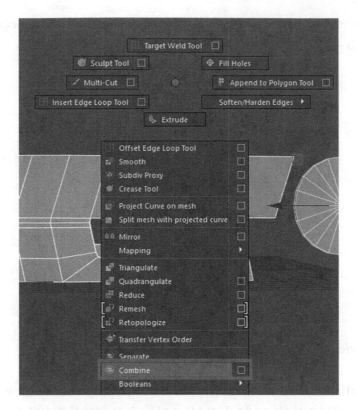

Figure 3-44. *Combining meshes*

After combining, go to edit mode and delete the faces shown in Figure 3-45.

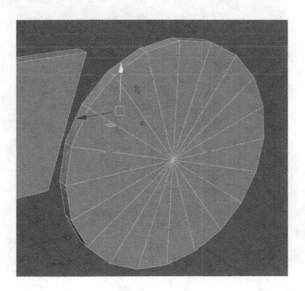

Figure 3-45. *Select and delete these faces*

Next, delete the face on the headpiece facing the cylinder. Then, select the edges shown in Figure 3-46.

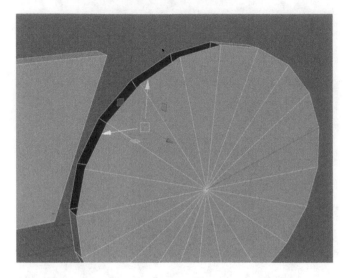

Figure 3-46. *Select these edges*

Then hold Shift and extrude the edges toward the headpiece. Next, switch to vertex mode. Press Shift+Right-click, and select Merge Vertices (see Figure 3-47).

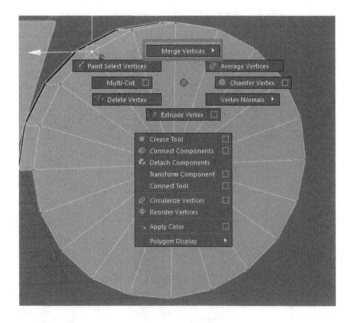

Figure 3-47. *Merge Vertices*

From the menu, select Target Weld Tool (see Figure 3-48).

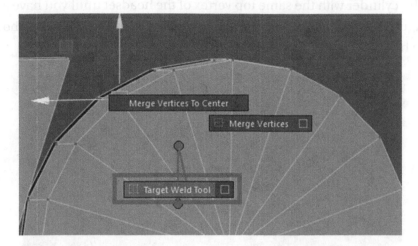

Figure 3-48. *Target Weld Tool*

Once enabled, your cursor changes to a + (plus-shaped) icon. This tool allows you to merge the selected vertex with a target vertex. It is very easy to use. First, select the vertex that you want to merge, and then select the target vertex where you want to merge it. In this case, select the top vertex on the extruded part of the cylinder, and then drag and drop it onto the adjacent vertex on the headset (see Figure 3-49).

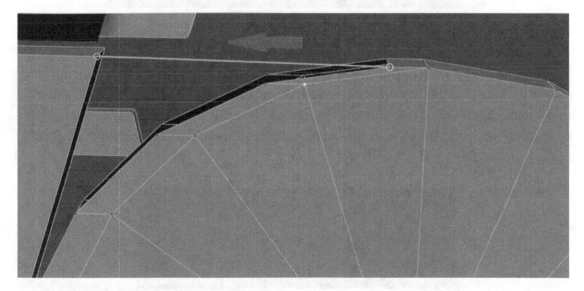

Figure 3-49. *Target welding vertices*

Do the same for all the vertices on one side of the cylinder: merge all the extruded vertices of the cylinder with the same top vertex of the headset until you have a result similar to Figure 3-50. Merge the very bottom vertex of the cylinder with the bottom vertex of the headset.

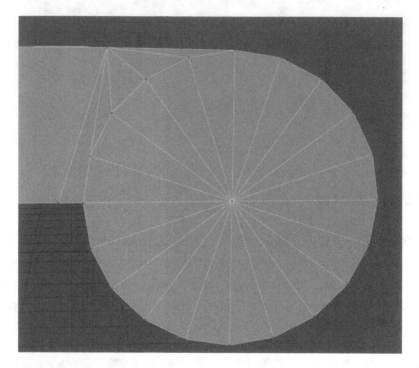

Figure 3-50. *The result after merging vertices*

You may find yourself in a situation where you have the cylindrical detail on only one side of the headset. If this is the case, you can mirror all the details from one side of the mesh to the other side. Make sure that your object is sitting on the grid and is not rotated at some weird angle. Once you have ensured all that, click the Mirror tool on the toolbar (see Figure 3-51).

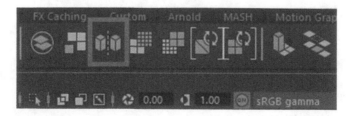

Figure 3-51. *Mirror tool*

The Mirror tool copies all the details from one side of the mesh to the other. If the result is not what you want, try rotating your object 90 degrees and mirror it again. Your results should look similar to Figure 3-52.

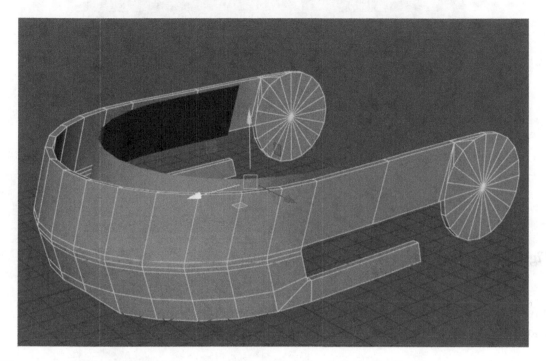

Figure 3-52. *Results so far*

Adding Details

Now let's add more details to our headset. Select all the faces on the cylinder and extrude them, as shown in Figure 3-53.

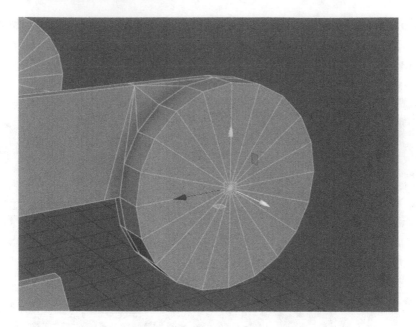

Figure 3-53. *Extruding the faces on the cylinder*

Extrude them again in a similar way. Press the R key to switch to the Scale tool. Use the central control point or the red square gizmo (both have the same effect), and then scale it down so that the shape is similar to what's shown in Figure 3-54.

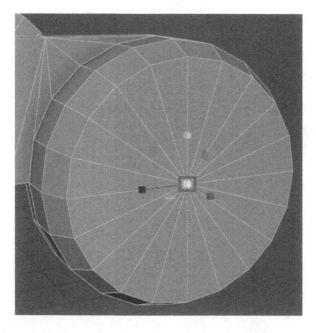

Figure 3-54. *Scaling down our shape using the Scale tool*

Go to the other side of the shape and select the highlighted edges, which are the cylinder's border edges (see Figure 3-55).

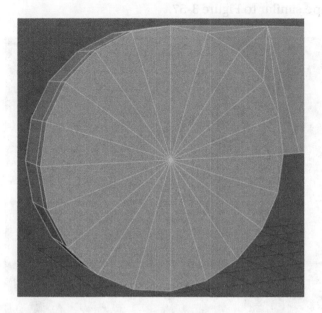

Figure 3-55. *Select these faces*

Duplicate these faces by pressing Shift+Right-click and selecting Duplicate faces in the menu. Scale down the faces so that they are similar to Figure 3-56.

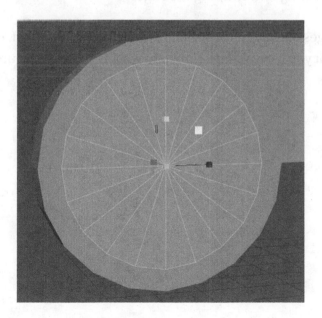

Figure 3-56. *Duplicate and scale the faces*

Next, select the shape's border edge loop and extrude by holding the Shift key and using the Move manipulator to extrude the edges outward. Scale the edges outward so that you have a shape similar to Figure 3-57.

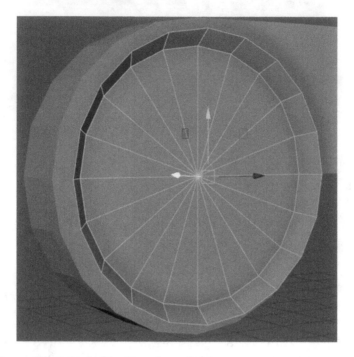

Figure 3-57. *Extruding and shaping the edges*

Extrude the edges outward once again in a straight line. After that, extrude and scale them inward so that you have a shape similar to what is shown in Figure 3-58. This is the *earpad*.

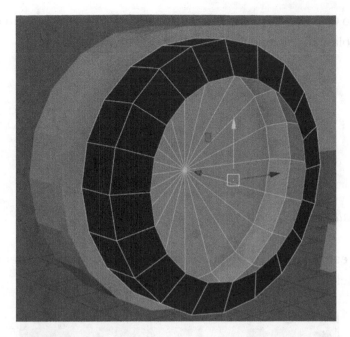

Figure 3-58. *Shape so far*

The faces are black because their normals are facing the wrong direction. Let's fix that before proceeding. Select all the faces, click the Mesh Display tab on the menu bar, and select Reverse in the menu (see Figure 3-59).

Figure 3-59. *Reversing normals*

Your mesh should now have the correct shading, and only the interior faces should be black.

Let's switch to Object mode for a moment. Click the Isolate Selection button (see Figure 3-60) to isolate the earpad (or press Shift+I, which is a shortcut).

Figure 3-60. *Isolate Selection button*

Now that the earpad is isolated, you can work on it without any other mesh in the way. Select and delete the backfaces of the earpad (see Figure 3-61).

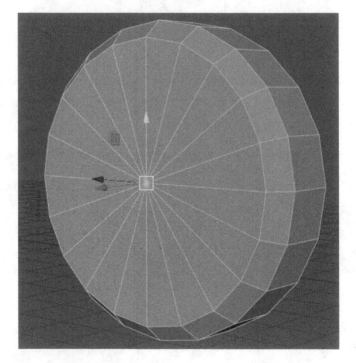

Figure 3-61. *Select and delete these faces*

Click the Isolate Selection button once again to reveal everything else.

Now, let's continue working on the earpad. Extrude, scale, and create a shape like the one shown in Figure 3-62.

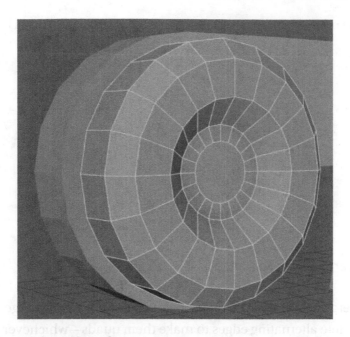

Figure 3-62. *Earpad result so far*

Select the very internal edge toward the center of the object. Extrude once again by holding the Shift key and using the Scale tool to extrude and scale down at the same time. This allows you close the hole in the center of the earpad. After that, press Shift+Right-click and select Merge/Collapse Edges (see Figure 3-63).

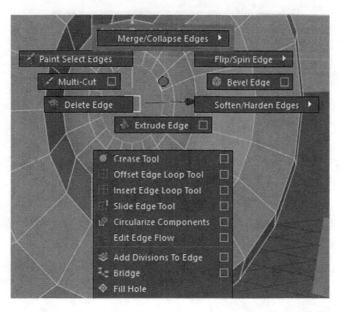

Figure 3-63. *Merge/Collapse Edges*

From the new menu, select Merge Edges To Center (see Figure 3-64).

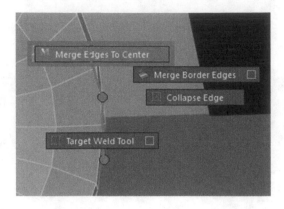

Figure 3-64. *Merge Edges To Center*

The edges merge at a central point. Triangles form where they merge. You can ignore that for now or delete alternating edges to make them quads—whichever you prefer. Game engines automatically triangulate meshes anyway, and for a flat hard surface, you can safely use triangles if they do not cause any issues with modeling. In our case, you can simply ignore them and move forward.

Add another edge loop as shown (dotted in green) in Figure 3-65 by pressing Shift+Right-click and selecting Insert Edge Loop Tool in the menu.

Figure 3-65. *Adding another edge loop*

Next, select the entire loop and move it out slightly to give the entire region a nice curve (see Figure 3-66).

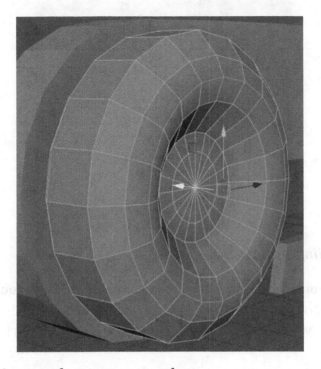

Figure 3-66. *Giving our shape some roundness*

Next, switch to face mode and press Ctrl+Shift+A to select all the faces and scale them upward so that the earpad is large enough to appear realistic; right now, it's too small. See Figure 3-67 for reference.

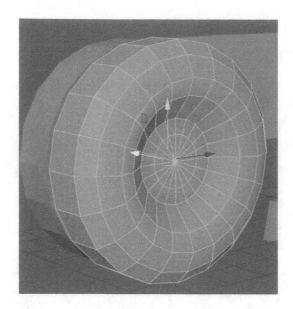

Figure 3-67. *Scaling and adjusting the size*

Now the size should look right, but you can adjust according to your preferences. Let's mirror it to the other side of the headset so that you have earpads on both sides. To do that, click the Mirror button on the toolbar. Your results should look similar to Figure 3-68.

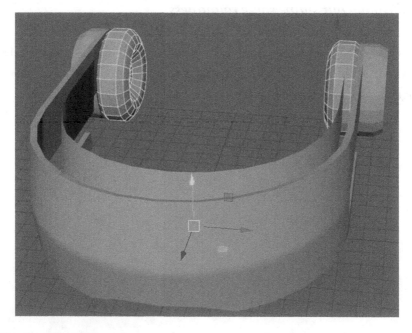

Figure 3-68. *Result of the mirror*

Isolating the Inner Object

Let's work on the inner headset. Isolate it first, and then switch to Edge Edit mode and add an edge loop, as shown in Figure 3-69.

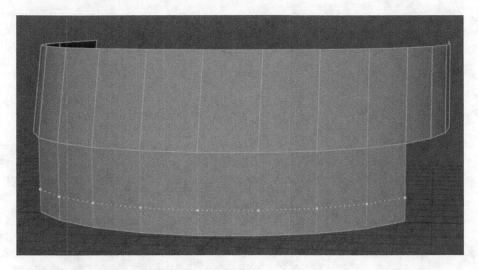

Figure 3-69. *Add edge loop as shown*

Now select the edges shown in Figure 3-70.

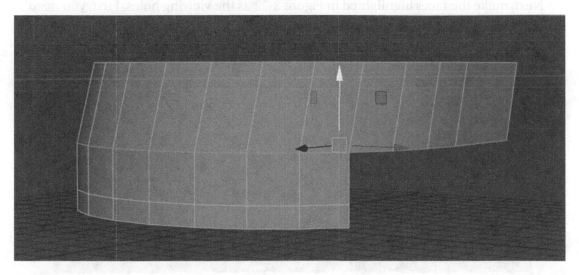

Figure 3-70. *Select the highlighted edges*

Press Shift+Ctrl, and using the Move manipulator, slide these edges upward to make the upper region of the mesh thinner. See Figure 3-71 for reference.

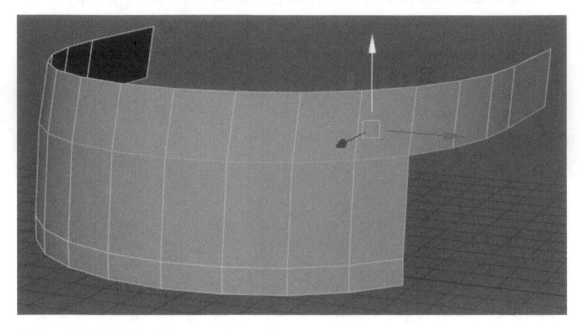

Figure 3-71. *Slide edges up*

Next, make the faces highlighted in Figure 3-72 as the viewing holes. First, you need to make changes in the geometries surrounding them.

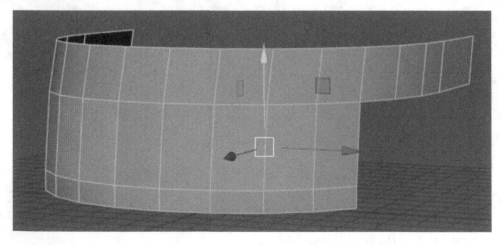

Figure 3-72. *Viewing holes*

Enable the Target Weld tool and merge the vertices with the corner vertex, as shown in Figure 3-73.

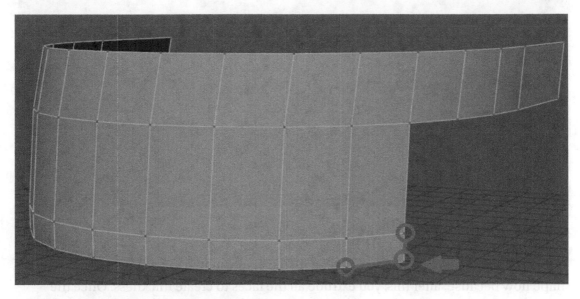

Figure 3-73. *Merge vertices to the corner*

Your results should look similar to Figure 3-74.

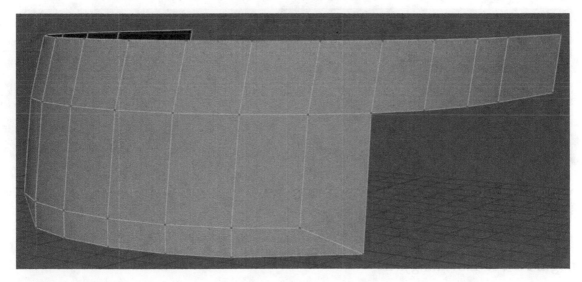

Figure 3-74. *Merged vertices at corner*

Next, select and delete the faces highlighted in Figure 3-75.

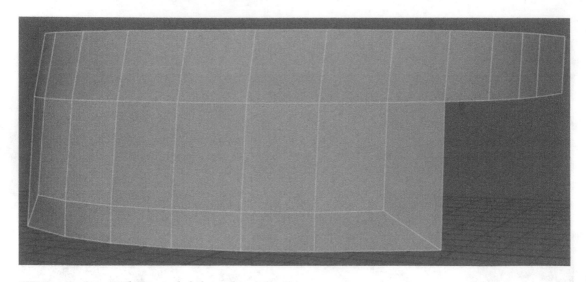

Figure 3-75. *Select and delete these faces*

You can adjust the shape more if needed. It is important to make any changes to the shape now because, after this, you extrude all the faces to create thickness. Once the thickness has been created, any further editing takes a lot of effort.

Select all the faces by pressing Ctrl+Shift+A. Go to Edit Mesh ➤ Extrude to extrude with the Thickness value set to 0.25. Your results should look similar to Figure 3-76.

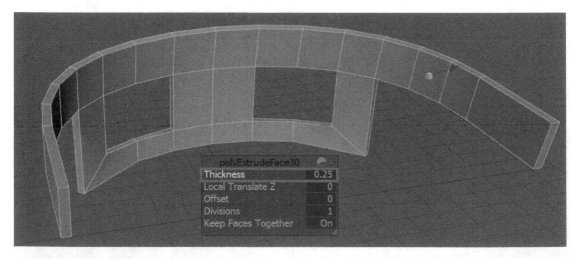

Figure 3-76. *Extruding faces*

Next, add an edge loop by pressing Ctrl+Right-click and selecting Insert Edge Loop Tool. Click to add an edge loop where it is highlighted in Figure 3-77.

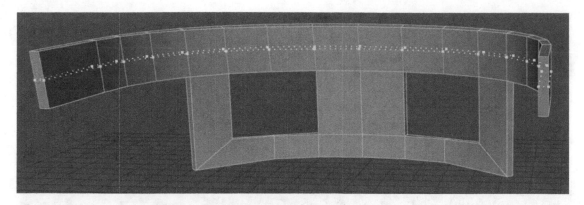

Figure 3-77. *Adding edge loop*

After that, select all the faces around the holes and extract them (see Figure 3-78).

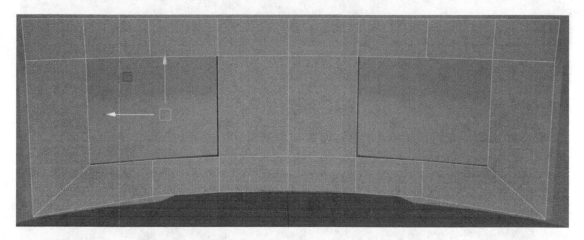

Figure 3-78. *Extract these faces*

Next, you extrude them with a value of 0.3. Your results should look similar to Figure 3-79.

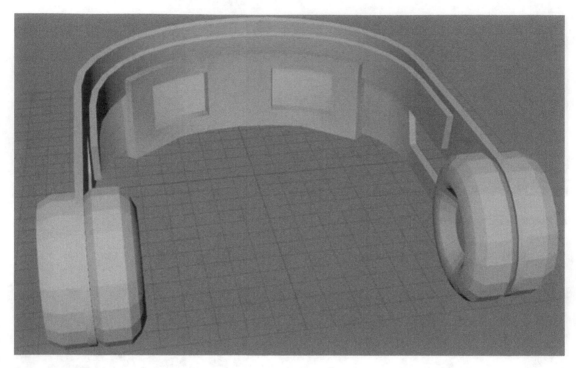

Figure 3-79.   *Result so far*

Select the faces highlighted in Figure 3-80 and duplicate them.

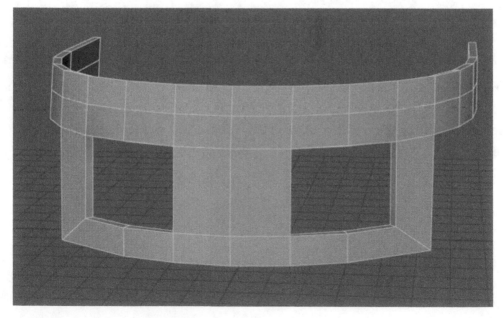

Figure 3-80.   *Select and duplicate these faces*

If you have problems working with duplicated faces, there is an alternative. First, press Ctrl+Z to undo any duplicating operations. Go to Object mode and clone the entire mesh by holding Shift and using the Translate tool. Then select and delete all the faces (by pressing the Backspace key) except the ones highlighted in Figure 3-80. This way, you don't have to deal with the Duplicate faces tool, which can be tricky to work with. After that, make sure to place the cloned mesh so that it roughly overlaps the original mesh.

Next, select all the vertices shown in Figure 3-81 and move them upward.

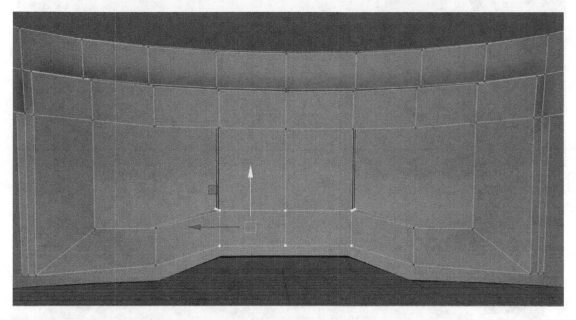

Figure 3-81. *Adjusting the shape of the object*

Once again, go to the Edge Edit mode of the duplicated faces and select the top edge highlighted in Figure 3-82. Slide them down slightly.

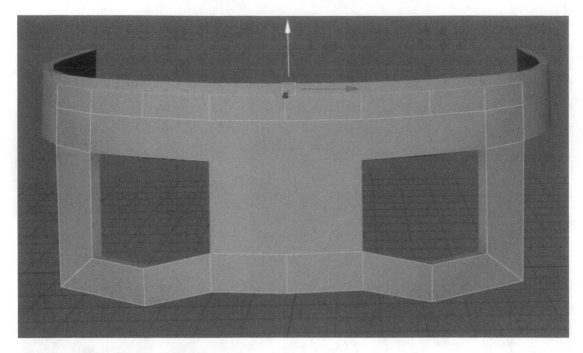

Figure 3-82. *Sliding edges down*

Do the same thing for all the border edges on this piece. Your results should look similar to Figure 3-83.

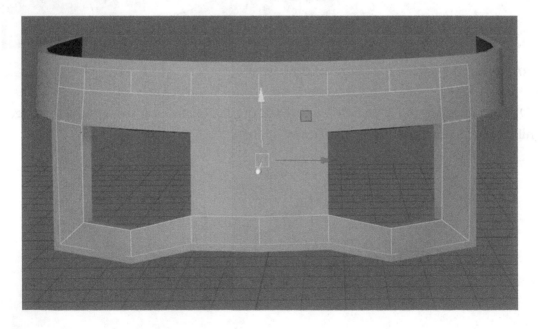

Figure 3-83. *Adjusting the border*

After adjusting the border, hold the Shift key and extrude the edges, as shown in Figure 3-84.

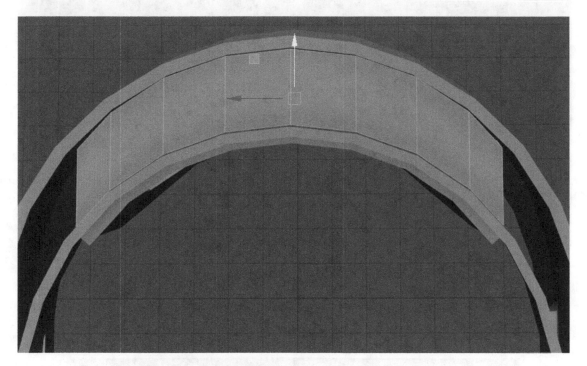

Figure 3-84. *Extrude the edges*

Removing Unwanted Faces

Some manual adjustment is required because some edges clip through the front part of the headset. Select them and move them back so that they are not sticking out from the front. There is no need to be too precise. After doing this, select and delete the mesh's backfaces (see Figure 3-85).

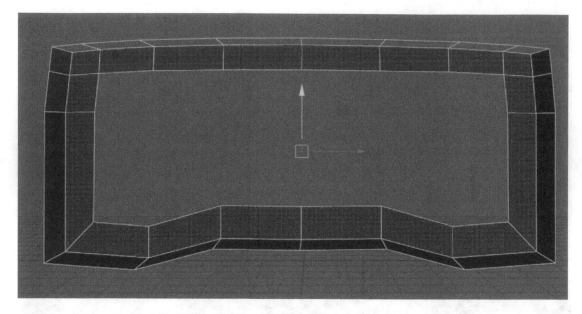

Figure 3-85. *Select and delete these faces*

Let's remove more unwanted faces. Select and isolate the mesh shown in Figure 3-86, and select the faces present on its convex side.

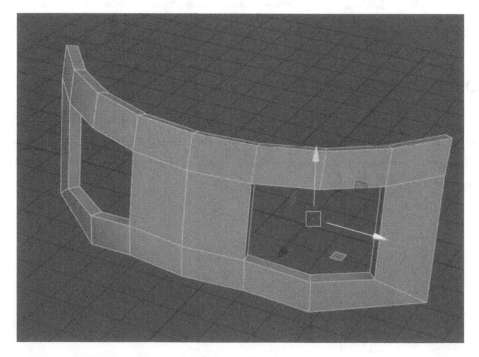

Figure 3-86. *Select these faces on this mesh*

And then delete them. You don't need these faces, and they won't be visible either, so it is better to just get rid of them (see Figure 3-87).

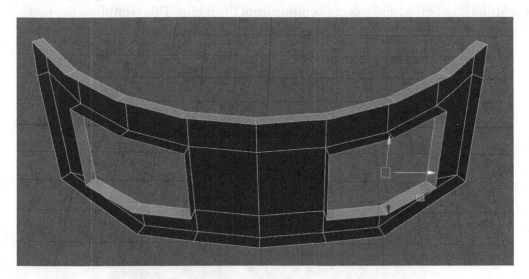

Figure 3-87. *Select these edge loops*

Making Final Adjustments

Press Shift+Right-click and select Fill Hole from the menu (see Figure 3-88). Let's create the eyepieces.

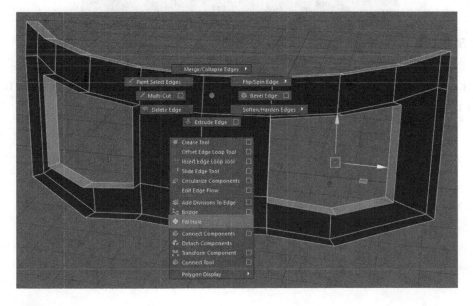

Figure 3-88. *Fill Hole*

This creates a new face. Select the new face, press Shift+Right-click, and select Extract Faces (see Figure 3-89). If the extracted faces are separate objects, select both, press Shift+Right-click, and select Combine from the menu. This combines the two meshes into one, and after that, you can enable Symmetry.

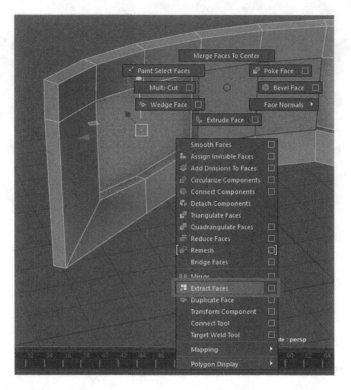

Figure 3-89. *Extracting Faces*

After extracting and combining, switch to vertex edit mode, and using a knife tool, connect the central top and bottom vertices (see Figure 3-90).

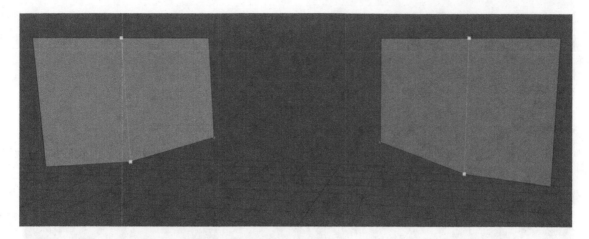

Figure 3-90. *Connecting the central vertices*

Next, go to the face edit mode and select all the faces. Click the Extrude tool in the toolbar (see Figure 3-91).

Figure 3-91. *Extrude tool*

Extrude with the Thickness value set to 0 and an Offset value set to 0.3 (see Figure 3-92).

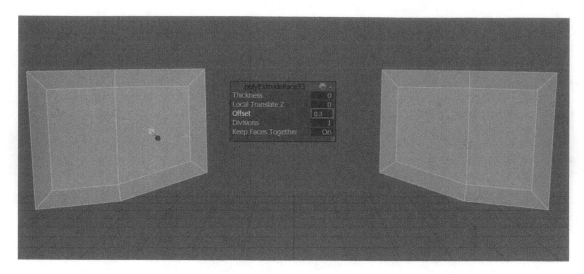

Figure 3-92. *Extruding with the Offset value*

Next, press Shift+Right-click again and select Circularize Components from the menu (see Figure 3-93).

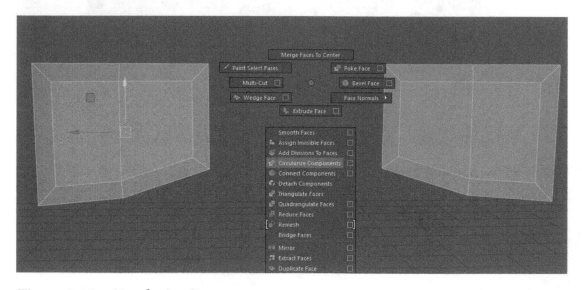

Figure 3-93. *Circularize Components*

Set Radial Offset to –0.4 (see Figure 3-94).

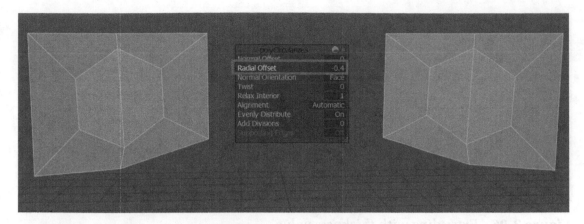

Figure 3-94. *Reducing Radial offset*

Extrude again with the Offset value set to 0.1 (see Figure 3-95).

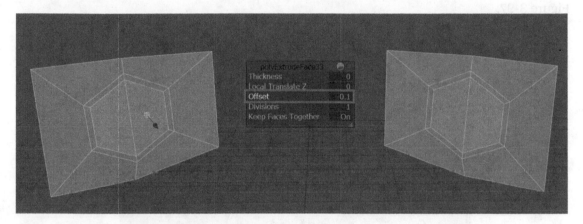

Figure 3-95. *Extruding with offset*

Extrude again with Offset set to 0 and Thickness set to 0.6 (see Figure 3-96).

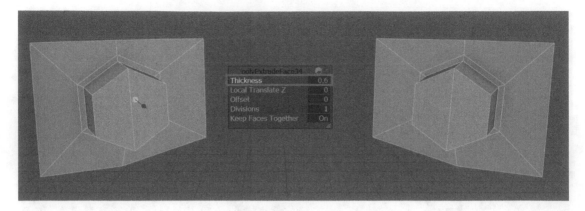

Figure 3-96. *Extruding with thickness value*

Extrude again with Offset set to 0.1 and Thickness set to 0. Finally, extrude one last time with Offset set to 0 and Thickness set to –0.5. You should have a shape similar to Figure 3-97.

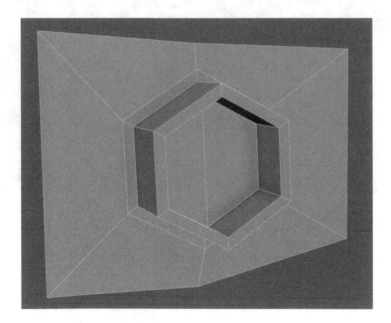

Figure 3-97. *Final shape*

Un-isolate everything and switch to the face edit mode of this mesh. Select all the faces by pressing Ctrl+Shift+A. Scale them up to fit the hole in a better way (see Figure 3-98) because currently, it appears to be too small.

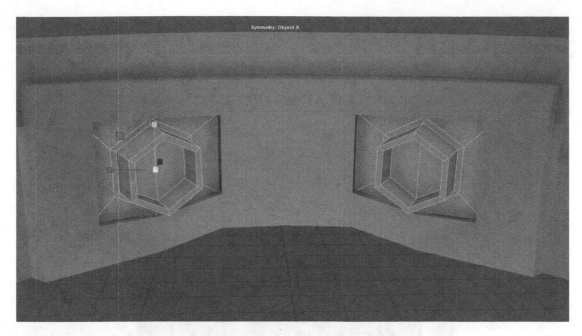

Figure 3-98. *Scaling our mesh*

Make sure to scale it up or down, depending on what you want. Your mesh may be different from mine, so make changes accordingly. With that, you are done with the basic blockout of the headset.

Let's make some slight changes to the overall shape and proportions. First, there is a gap between the two meshes, as visible in Figure 3-99.

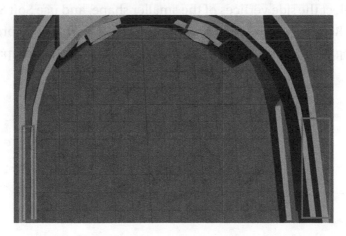

Figure 3-99. *Gaps between meshes*

Fix this by selecting the smaller mesh and scale it along the Z – X plane using the Scale tool (see Figure 3-100). This may not be the best method because the mesh gets squished in proportions. An alternative method is described in the next step.

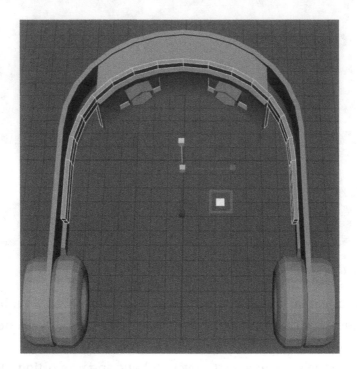

Figure 3-100. *Scale using the Z – X plane handle*

Or you can select the side vertices of the smaller shape, and use Soft Selection to adjust the shape. Remember, you can enable/disable Soft Selection by pressing the B key. After enabling, select the vertices shown in Figure 3-101 and move part of the mesh sideways.

Figure 3-101. *Adjust shape using Soft Selection*

Also adjust any other part of the mesh that is affected because other regions can get misaligned. Afterward, increase the thickness of the part highlighted in Figure 3-102. Currently, it appears to be too thin.

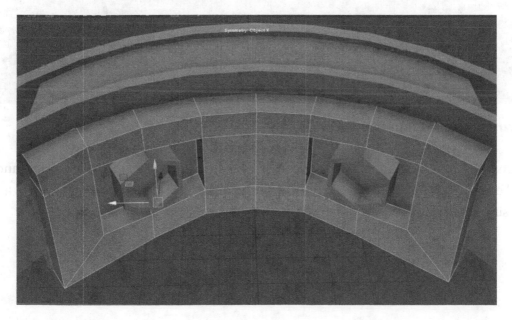

Figure 3-102. *Making the mesh thicker*

Final adjustments are up to you. If you think a certain part of the mesh needs to be adjusted, then do as you choose. Make sure not to make any drastic changes to the overall shape or design unless you're confident about what you are doing.

Starting the Detailing Phase

Once you are done with the adjustment phase, you begin the detailing phase. In this section, you start adding details to our mesh and make it look better. You start with the very front mesh. Select it and press the alphanumeric 3 key to enable the subdivided mesh display. Your mesh should appear similar to Figure 3-103 after pressing 3.

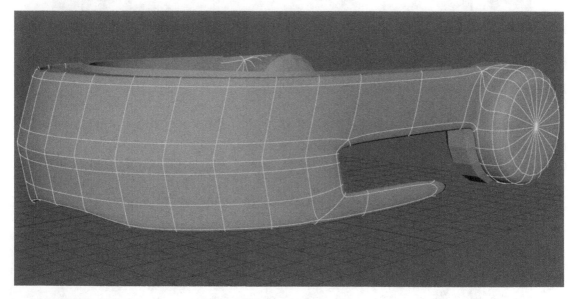

Figure 3-103. *Subdivided mesh display*

As you can now see, the mesh appears smooth and has lost all the hard corners and hard edges. You can enable this for all the mesh pieces by selecting them one by one and pressing 3. This subdivides them (see Figure 3-104).

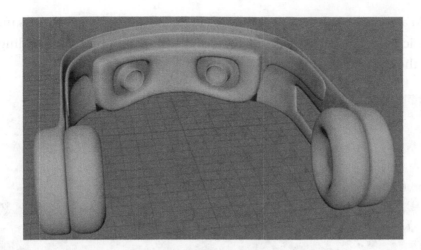

Figure 3-104. *Subdivided display of our headset*

It may not look good now, but add supporting edge loops and bring back the hard edges. It is a good visualization as you work and add details. For detailing work, you are adding a lot of edge loops. Let's review how to do that because it is an integral part of this phase. If you have black-colored backfaces with reversed normals, it's distracting. Select the object with backfaces, then go to Display ➤ Polygons ➤ Backface Culling. This stops the backfaces from rendering. You can disable it by clicking Backface Culling again.

To add an edge loop, simply press Shift+Right-click, and select Insert Edge Loop Tool (see Figure 3-105).

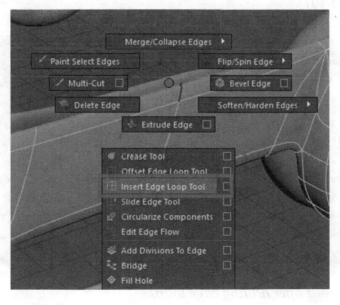

Figure 3-105. *Insert Edge Loop Tool*

Let's add a couple of edge loops, as shown in Figure 3-106. You can press the alphanumeric 1 key to disable the subdivided view if you have problems adding an edge loop due to the curvature of the mesh.

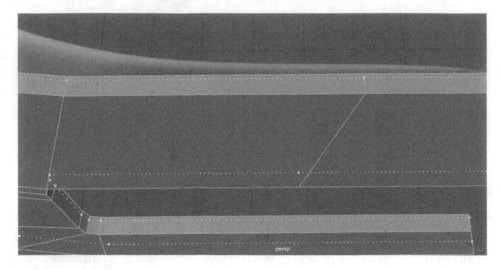

Figure 3-106. *Adding edge loop*

And as you can see, you are adding the edge loop very close to the border edge. This ensures that when you subdivide the mesh, that place has a harder angle. Let's add another edge to the other side very close to the border edge. Press 3 again to see the result (see Figure 3-107).

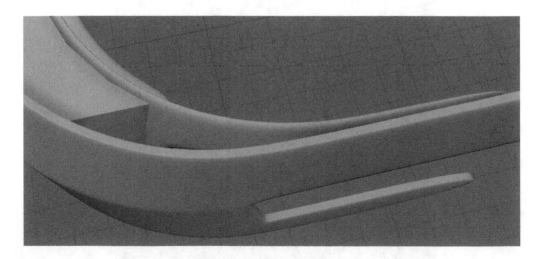

Figure 3-107. *Result after adding edge loops*

As you can see, the angles are harder now, and the mesh looks much better. These types of edges are called *supporting edge loops* because they support the object's shape so that the Subdivide function doesn't make the mesh too smooth.

Let's add some supporting edge loops to the lower part of the front headset piece. Add a couple of edge loops, as shown in Figure 3-108.

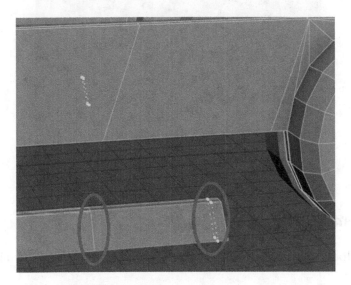

Figure 3-108. *Add a couple of edge loops as shown*

After adding the edge loops, press 3 and look at the results. You see that the lower parts of the front headset piece now hold on better. This is exactly what you want.

Add supporting edges to places where you want to preserve the hard angles (any place where an angle is becoming too rounded). I added a couple to the highlighted region (see Figure 3-109).

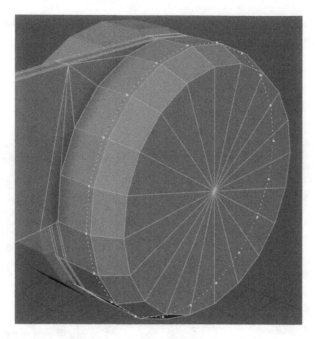

Figure 3-109. *Adding support edge loop here*

Add another loop to the other side. Then add a couple more, as shown in Figure 3-110.

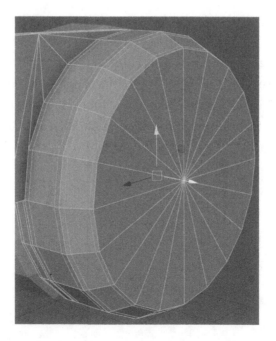

Figure 3-110. *Adding supporting edge loops*

If you press 3, your results should look similar to Figure 3-111.

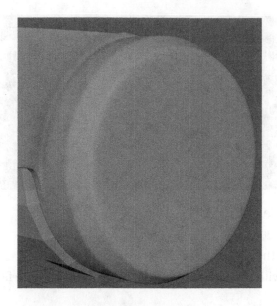

Figure 3-111. *Result after supporting edge loops*

On the side of the mesh, you see that the triangles present on the flat face prevent you from adding supporting edges. To get around that, first, select all the faces, as shown in Figure 3-112.

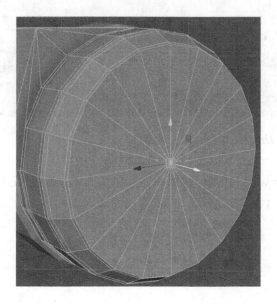

Figure 3-112. *Select these faces*

Then extrude the faces with the parameters shown in Figure 3-113.

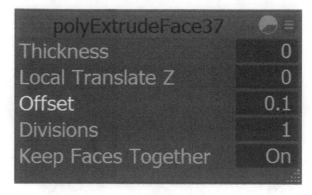

Figure 3-113. *Extrude settings*

Press 3 and look at the results.

Let's do the same with the front part of the visor. Select all the faces shown in Figure 3-114.

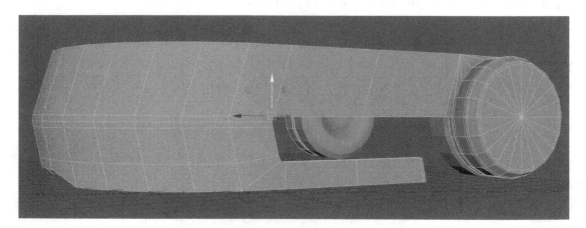

Figure 3-114. *Select these faces*

Extrude these faces with Offset set to 0.05 and Thickness set to 0. You should get a result similar to Figure 3-115.

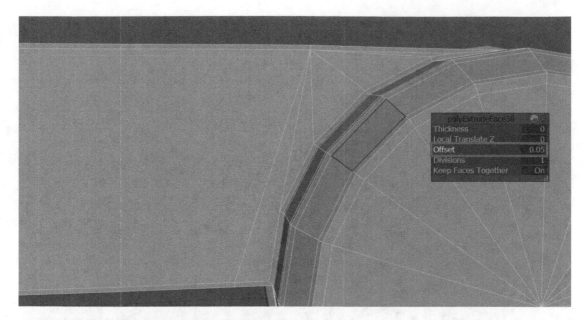

Figure 3-115. *Extruding with offset*

If you press 3, the subdivided view has very nice sharp angles, and the shape does not collapse. Let's do the same thing for the back part. Select all the faces and extrude with Offset set to 0.09 (see Figure 3-116).

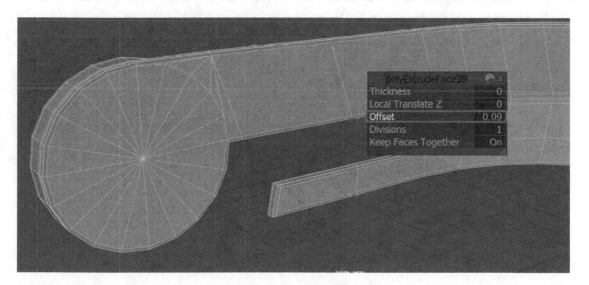

Figure 3-116. *Extruding the back region with offset*

Add one more edge loop, as shown in Figure 3-117.

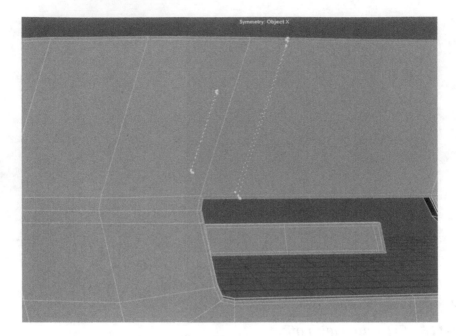

Figure 3-117. *Adding another edge loop*

Most of the work is done on the front part of the headpiece. You only need to solve one final problem. Look at the front of the mesh where you created a design by pulling the faces upward. Applying subdivision rounds off the shape, and you don't want that; but if you try to add supporting edge loops, the shape gets hard angles that you don't want either. Try it and see what happens.

Correcting Angle Problems

To get around the angle problem, you must make changes to the Insert Edge Loop tool. First, press Shift+Right-click and click the small square icon next to the Insert Edge Loop Tool name (see Figure 3-118).

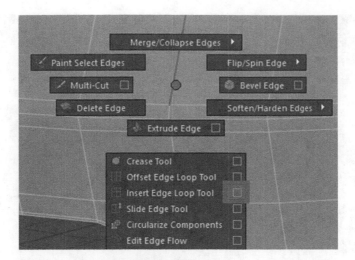

Figure 3-118. *Insert Edge Loop Tool options*

In the Tool Settings window, set Maintain Position to Multiple Edge Loops and set Number of Edge Loops to 1 (see Figure 3-119).

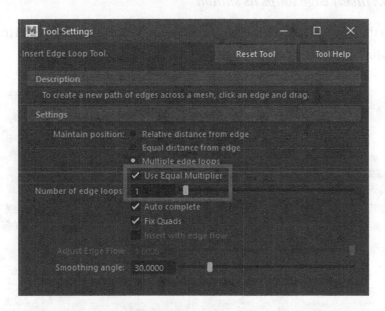

Figure 3-119. *Tool settings for Insert Edge Loop tool*

When you insert an edge loop, it is inserted exactly in the center of the region. Insert four edge loops, as highlighted in Figure 3-120.

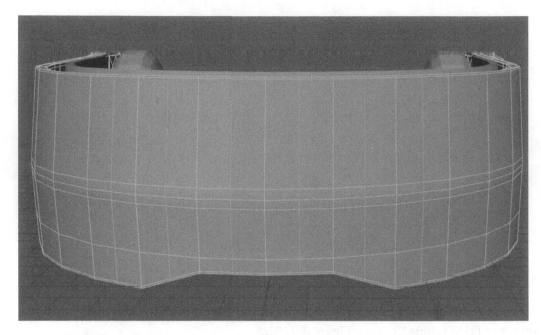

Figure 3-120. *Insert edge loops as shown*

Next, go to the top view by holding the spacebar, clicking Maya in the Hotbar, and selecting Top from the pie menu (see Figure 3-121).

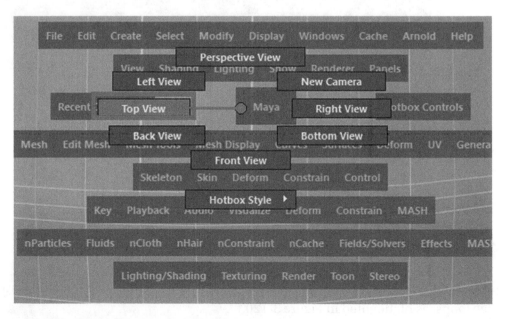

Figure 3-121. *Switching to top view*

In the top view, make sure that the edge loops you added are selected (see Figure 3-122) and note how the entire region appears flat.

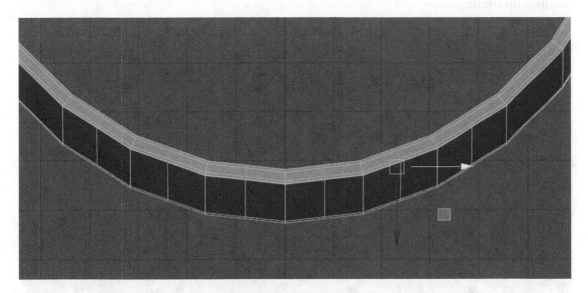

Figure 3-122. *Make sure these loops are selected*

You need to remove this flatness because when you subdivide the mesh, the flatness is visible—and you don't want that. You want this region to be smooth. To fix this, move the edges slightly outward (see Figure 3-123).

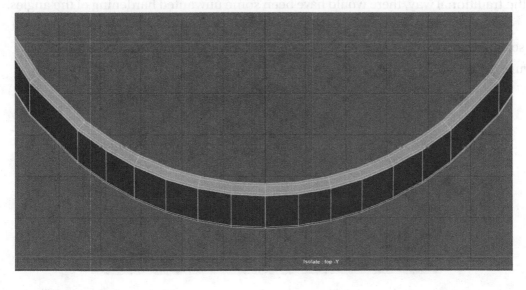

Figure 3-123. *Giving our shape a curve*

By manually moving the edge loops out, you have removed the flatness and reintroduced the smooth curve. And as you can see in Figure 3-124, the design is now holding up better.

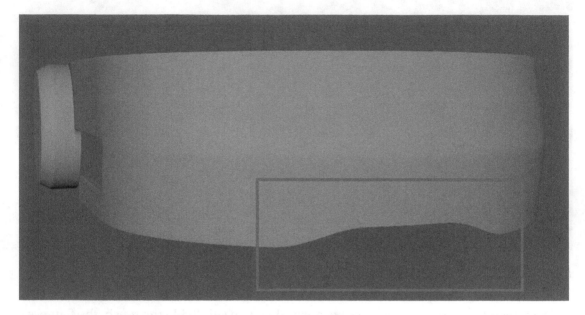

Figure 3-124. *Shape after adding supporting edges*

As you can see, the shape has some hardness now. Had we added supporting edges in the traditional way, there would have been some unwanted hardening of the angles.

Now let's work on another part of the headset. Before you add edge loops, let reset its settings. Press Shift+Right-click and select the Insert Edge Loop Tool settings (see Figure 3-125).

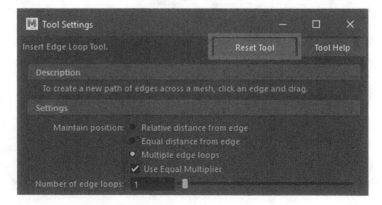

Figure 3-125. *Tool settings*

First, add a couple of supporting edge loops, as shown in Figure 3-126.

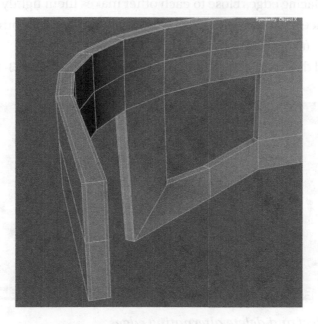

Figure 3-126. *Insert a couple of edge loops as shown*

Add additional supporting edges to all the meshes, and the result should look similar to Figure 3-127.

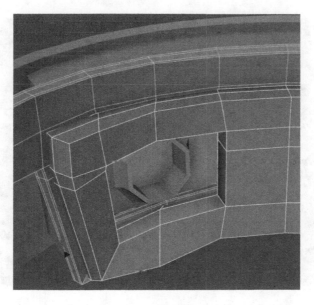

Figure 3-127. *Placement of supporting edge loops*

As you can see, I placed the supporting edge toward the center because I wanted this region softer. Placing edges close to each other makes them tightly subdivided, but having some distance makes the subdivision more relaxed and smoother. You can use this information to customize the hardness.

Next, select and delete the alternating edges, as shown in Figure 3-128.

Figure 3-128. Select and delete alternating edges

Next, while in any Edge Edit mode, press Ctrl+Shift+A to select every edge in the mesh. Then go to Mesh Display ➤ Soften/Harden Edges and click the small square button to open the tool options. Increase Angle from 30 to 180 degrees (see Figure 3-129).

Figure 3-129. Softening the edges

Click Apply to apply softening edges. Your mesh should now look smoother, as shown in Figure 3-130.

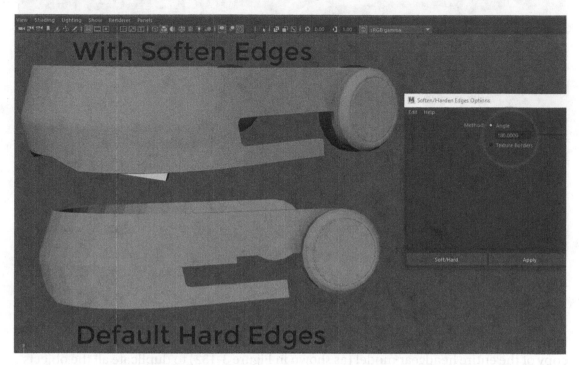

Figure 3-130.   *Hard and soft edges*

Doing a Shader Test

Let's do a quick Shader test (see Figure 3-131). Right-click and go to Assign New Material. Then apply Lambert. In the Attribute Editor, apply a slight color variation. This is an optional step, so no need to worry too much about it.

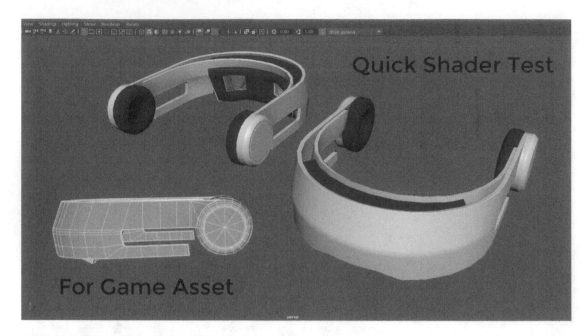

Figure 3-131. *Doing a quick Shader test*

With supporting edge loops applied to all the meshes, first select everything by pressing Ctrl+Shift+A. Then hold the Shift key, and using any Move manipulator, create a copy of the entire headgear model (as shown in Figure 3-132) to duplicate all the objects in your project.

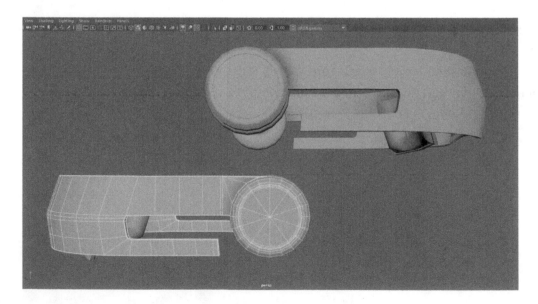

Figure 3-132. *Duplicating the entire model*

Place it high to not interfere with the model that you're working with. Then, select any piece of the lower model and apply the Smooth option by clicking Mesh ➤ Smooth (see Figure 3-133).

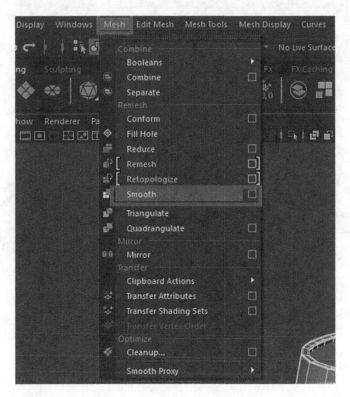

Figure 3-133. *Applying smooth*

In the Smooth options window, set Divisions to 1 (see Figure 3-134).

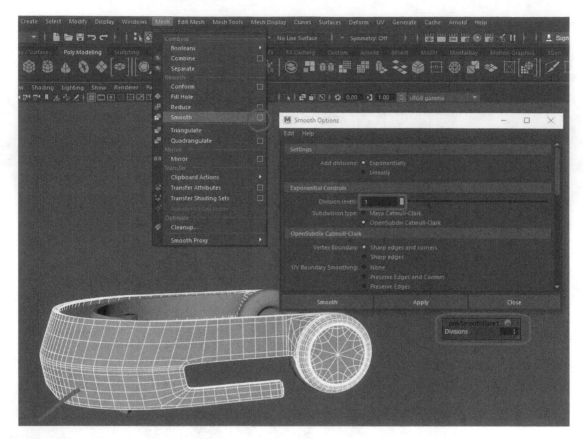

Figure 3-134. *Applying smooth to the mesh*

Reducing Poly Count

Next, manually select and delete the edge loops to bring down the poly count to acceptable amounts. Select the edge loops as shown in Figure 3-135, and delete them by pressing Ctrl+Backspace.

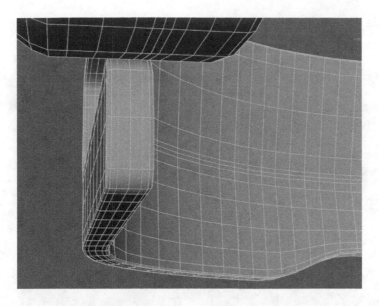

Figure 3-135. *Select these edge loops*

Next, select and delete the edge loops highlighted in Figure.

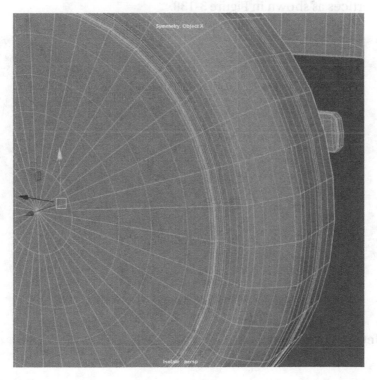

Figure 3-136. *Select and delete these edges*

Next, enable the Target Weld tool and merge all the highlighted vertices, as shown in Figure 3-137.

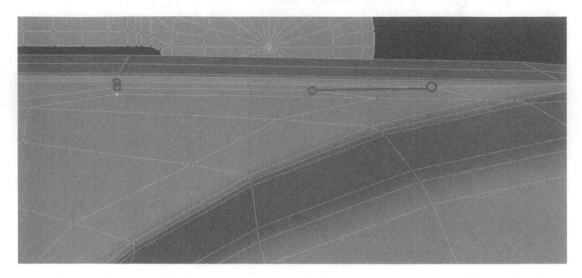

Figure 3-137.   *Merge these vertices, bottom one to the top one*

Merge the vertices as shown in Figure 3-138.

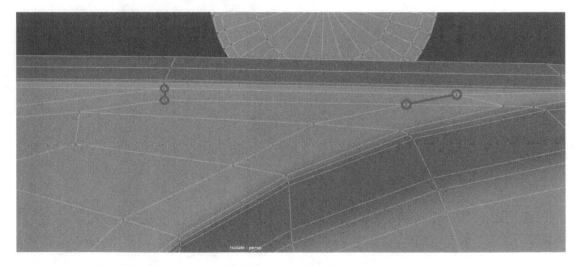

Figure 3-138.   *Merge vertices as shown, bottom one to top one*

Finally, delete the highlighted edge shown in Figure 3-139.

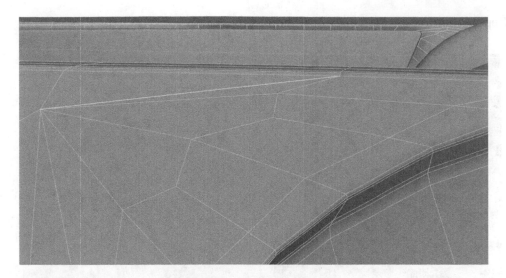

Figure 3-139. *Select and delete the highlighted edge*

Let's reduce the polygon count for the other meshes as well. Select and delete all the edges, as shown in Figure 3-140.

Figure 3-140 shows that we successfully reduced the polycount of the asset to an amount that even weaker PCs can bake. Let's do the same for other assets.

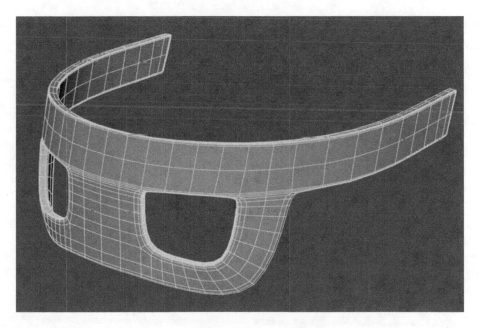

Figure 3-140. *Reduced polycount of asset*

Repeat the process until you have something similar to Figure 3-141.

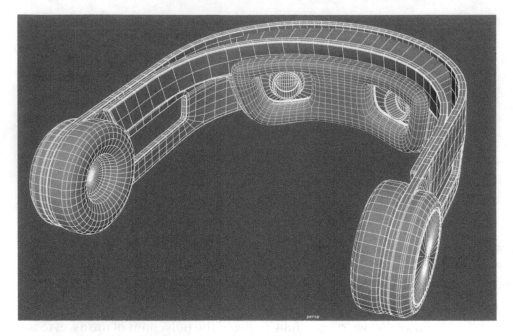

Figure 3-141. *Mesh with reduced polygon count*

You can use it for baking mesh maps in Substance Painter. Figure 3-142 shows the topology of the low poly mesh. It accepts our high poly details with no problems.

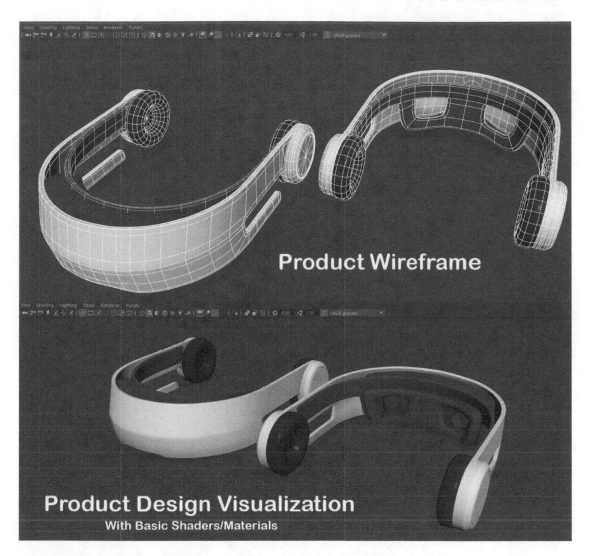

Figure 3-142. *Our low poly model*

This model still has a high number of polygons, so use it as a high poly mesh when baking mesh maps in Substance Painter. Make sure to keep the original mesh; it serves as a low poly mesh on which you bake everything.

As you can see, certain parts of the mesh have been left untouched, which is fine. You don't want to destroy any details because they affect the texture bake.

The next chapter explores the basics of Unreal Engine 4.

CHAPTER 4

Interactive Visualization with UE4

Unreal Engine 4 is a game engine for building games, architectural walkthroughs, product visualizations, and more using assets and codes. They can be released on any supported platform. UE4 is a very popular game engine. Many AAA developers and indie studios use it to create modern games. Nowadays, if someone wants a job in the game industry, a portfolio that includes UE4 skills is highly recommended.

The Unreal Engine 4 Interface

Let's start with the basics of Unreal Engine 4. First, let's look at how to open it. Open the Epic Games Launcher and browse to the Unreal Engine section (see Figure 4-1).

Figure 4-1. *Switching to the Unreal Engine section*

A. Kumar, *Immersive 3D Design Visualization*, https://doi.org/10.1007/978-1-4842-6597-0_4

Under the Library tab, there is a plus icon. Click it to add a version of UE4 to your library. Next, click the Install button and select your directory to start the UE4 installation (see Figure 4-2). Always download the latest version so that you can use the latest features.

Figure 4-2. *Installing UE4 version*

Figure 4-2 shows that UE4 version 4.25.3 is installed and ready to launch. (Version 4.24.3 was not downloaded, so the Install button is still showing.)

Launch the version of the engine that you installed by clicking the Launch button. In the new window that opens, create a first-person project by selecting With Starter Content and its settings, as shown in Figure 4-3.

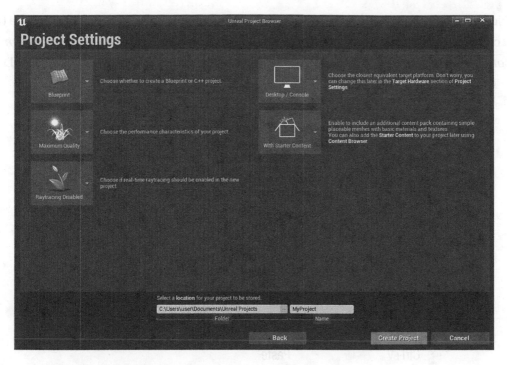

Figure 4-3. *Default settings*

And after creating a project, the first window that you see is shown in Figure 4-4.

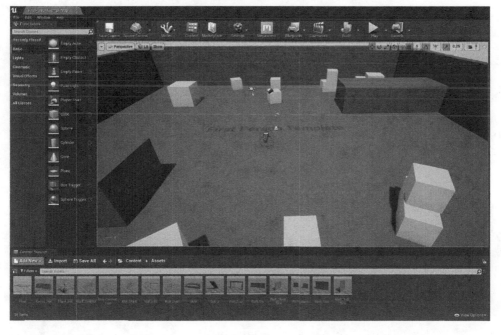

Figure 4-4. *The Unreal Engine 4 interface*

Now, let's discuss the basic controls in UE4. You can press Alt+Left-click to *rotate* the view camera. Press Alt+Middle-click to *pan* the camera. Press Alt+Right-click to *zoom in and out*. Alternatively, you can hold Right-click and fly around with the W, S, A, and D keys. Table 4-1 lists some of the important Unreal Engine 4 hotkeys.

Table 4-1. *Important Unreal Engine 4 Hotkeys*

Hotkey	Effect
W	Translate
E	Rotate
R	Scale
Ctrl+A	Select all
Ctrl+X	Cut
Ctrl+C	Copy
Ctrl+V	Paste
Del	Delete
Ctrl+W	Duplicate
Ctrl+Z	Undo
Ctrl+Y	Redo
F2	Rename
F	Focus
Alt+G	Perspective view
Alt+H	Front view
Alt+K	Side view
Alt+J	Top view
Alt+P	Play world
F11	Immersive mode
G	Game view

(*continued*)

Table 4-1. (*continued*)

Hotkey	Effect
End	Snap to floor
Ctrl+S	Save all
Ctrl+Shift+S	Save current

On the left side of the viewport is the Place Actors panel (see Figure 4-5). In UE4, everything that you place in the world is an actor with components attached to them to dictate their behavior.

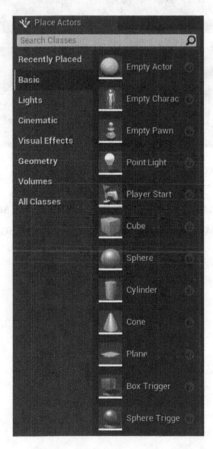

Figure 4-5. *Place Actors window*

The Content Browser is at the bottom of the screen (see Figure 4-6). It is the UE4 file browser. It shows you everything that you have imported or created for your game, including assets, codes, blueprints, and so forth.

Before proceeding, you need to know about Blueprints and why it is a game-changer for people who are not very familiar with programming. Blueprints is a node-based visual programming language that allows UE4 users to create gameplay logic using nodes without writing a single line of code. You can even make an entire game only using Blueprints, which is good for visualization. A bigger game should not be created by only using Blueprints because it is not that optimized. Still, a lot of gameplay logic is made with Blueprints, so it is very useful.

Figure 4-6. *Content Browser*

The World Outliner is on the top-right side of the screen (see Figure 4-7). It lists every actor that you placed in the world, including assets, lights, visual effects, volumes, and so forth.

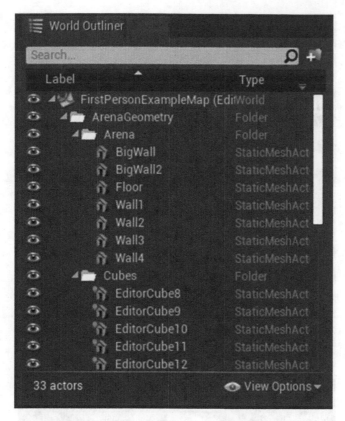

Figure 4-7. *World Outliner*

The Details panel is on the bottom-right side of your screen (see Figure 4-8). This panel features the properties and editable parameters of a selected asset in the world.

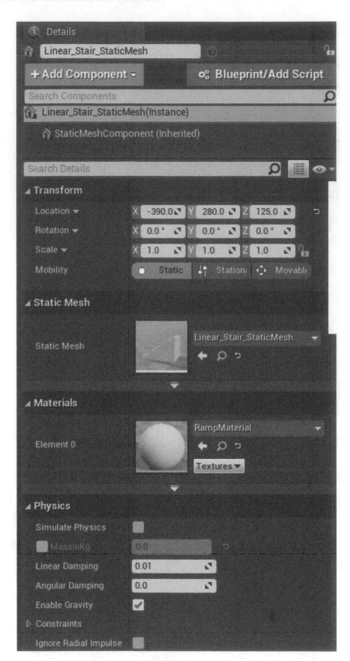

Figure 4-8. *Details panel*

The toolbar is at the center top of the screen. It features the tools that are most used as you work on your project (see Figure 4-9).

Figure 4-9. *UE4 toolbar*

Level Editor

The Level Editor is a core UE4 editor. It allows users to manage and edit levels. Levels are created and edited by placing and editing Actors in a scene. These actors define what any player will experience when interacting with that level and its actors. To open the Level Editor, go to Window ➤ Levels (see Figure 4-10).

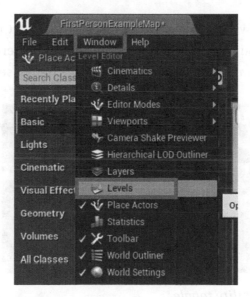

Figure 4-10. *Opening the Levels panel*

Once the Levels panel is open, you see the window shown in Figure 4-11.

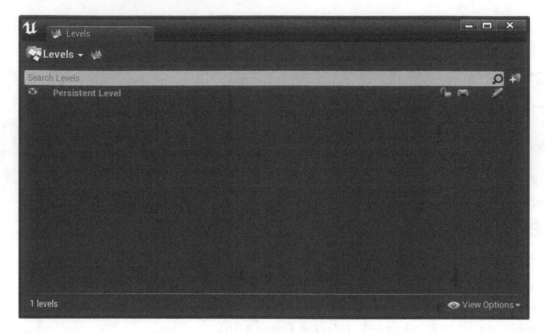

Figure 4-11. *Levels window*

The Levels panel shows all the levels present in your scene. Currently, the default example level is open. You can see that this window is named Persistent Level. You can disable this level by clicking the open eye icon before its name (see Figure 4-12).

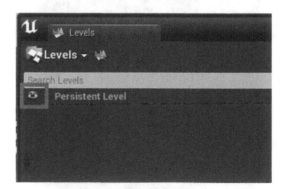

Figure 4-12. *Level visibility toggle*

Once you disable a level, everything in the scene disappears. This shows that every actor in your scene is a part of a level. By editing these actors, you modify the level. You can save your changes by clicking the pencil icon in the right corner of the window (see Figure 4-13).

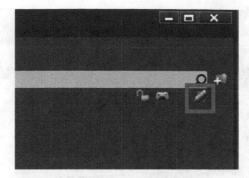

Figure 4-13. *Saving changes in a level*

A floppy disk icon is shown when there are no new changes to save.

Output Log

The Output Log panel is a developer tool that displays debug messages and error messages related to what's happening in the background. Error messages are logged here, which provides valuable information on what went wrong so that you can investigate and fix problems. To open the output log, go to Windows ➤ Developer Tools ➤ Output Log (see Figure 4-14).

Figure 4-14. *Opening the output log*

Once the output log is open, you should see that there are many messages related to everything that you have done in the backend of the engine (see Figure 4-15).

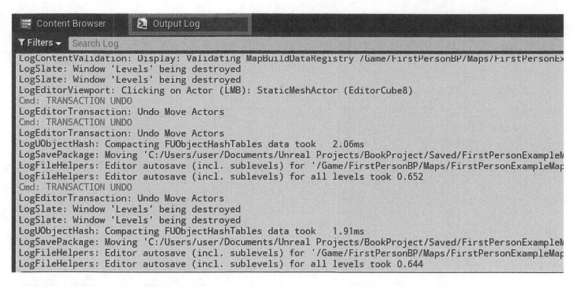

Figure 4-15. Output log

Now you have seen the UE4 interface, and we will explore all the tools in detail as you use them. Don't get too overwhelmed by the amount of information in this chapter. You usually don't need to use every tool and parameter; if you know how to properly use the most common tools, you can easily create whatever you want. As for the rest, the more you practice, the more you practise the more proficient you become. Try everything out in a test scene. The next chapter discusses how to create assets for our project.

CHAPTER 5

Creating Virtual Worlds

In this chapter, you create a level by using some very basic shapes created in Maya. This will be our white-box level, which serves as a foundation for what you are trying to make.

Creating the Asset Library

Since you have already done modelling work, there won't be any step-by-step tutorial for the simple blockout shapes. Figure 5-1 shows the asset library that you are using for this project.

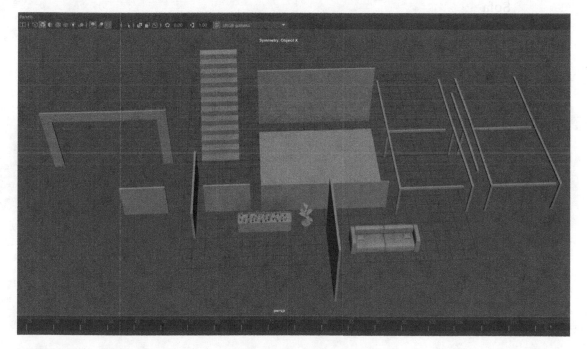

Figure 5-1. *Asset library*

© Abhishek Kumar 2021

A. Kumar, *Immersive 3D Design Visualization*, https://doi.org/10.1007/978-1-4842-6597-0_5

Creating a Basic Level Layout

As you can see in Figure 5-1, there is nothing fancy in this scene; it has very simple geometric shapes.

Here is a list of the assets that you have, all exported in FBX format.

Floor

Grass_Pot

Plant_Pot

Rail_Central

Rail_Mid

Rail_Main

Rail_Central_End

Rail_Side

Sofa

Stairs

Wall_Door

Wall_Short

Wall_Short_Side

Wall_Split

Wall_High

Wall_High_Side

Let's begin by creating a new empty scene in UE4. First, click File and then click New Level (see Figure 5-2).

Figure 5-2. *Creating a new level*

In the New Level window, select Default (see Figure 5-3).

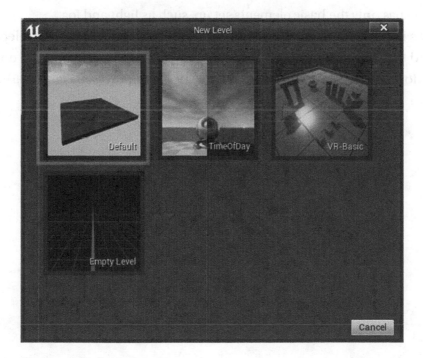

Figure 5-3. *Create a default level*

Your new basic level should look like Figure 5-4.

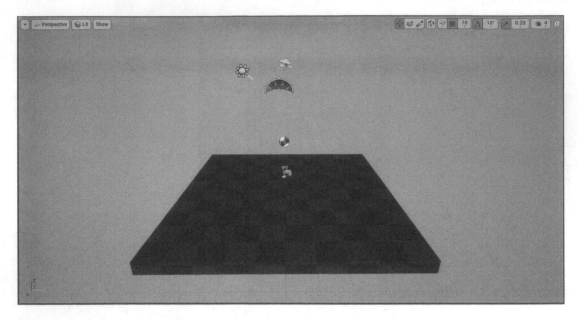

Figure 5-4. *New default level*

This level has only the basic elements set up, such as light and fog.

Now let's import our assets and get started. To import an asset, simply select it in Explorer and then drag and drop it into the UE4 Content Browser. When you do this, an import window opens, giving you many options for file import (see Figure 5-5).

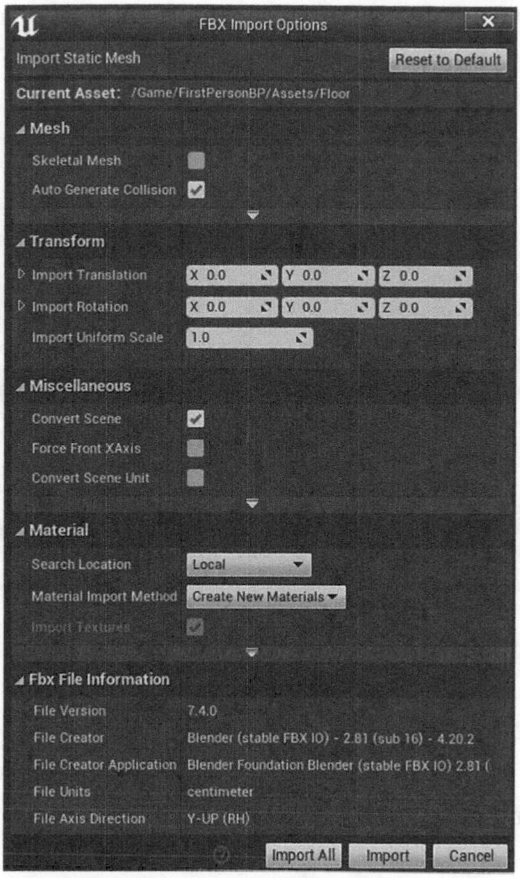

Figure 5-5. *Import options for assets*

You are not going to change anything for now, so leave everything at default. Click the Import All button. Once your assets have been imported, put them in a folder named Assets to keep everything organized. The location should be Content ➤ FirstPersonBP ➤ Assets. And now you have assets in UE4 (see Figure 5-6).

Figure 5-6. *Our assets in the Content Browser*

Next, you need to save this level. Press Ctrl+S to initiate save. In the Save Level As window, name your level appropriately, and then click Save (see Figure 5-7).

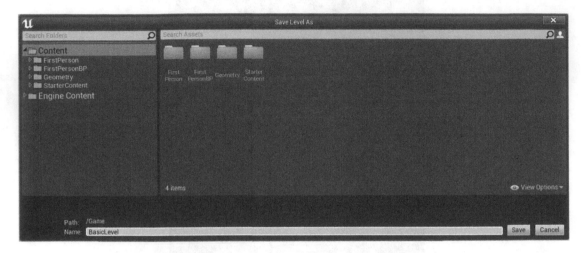

Figure 5-7. *Save window*

Next, let's drag and drop the Floor asset from the Content Browser into the scene. Set its Location to 0.0 on all the axes in the Details Window (see Figure 5-8). This gives our asset a location of 0,0,0 in the 3D space, which means the center of the world.

Figure 5-8. *Setting the asset location*

When editing values in the input fields of any parameter, you can press the Tab key to quickly switch between the different property fields. This allows you to quickly edit the values.

Next, delete the default floor that was present in the scene. Then, add the Floor asset to the scene in the 0,0,0 location. Now you should have a scene similar to Figure 5-9.

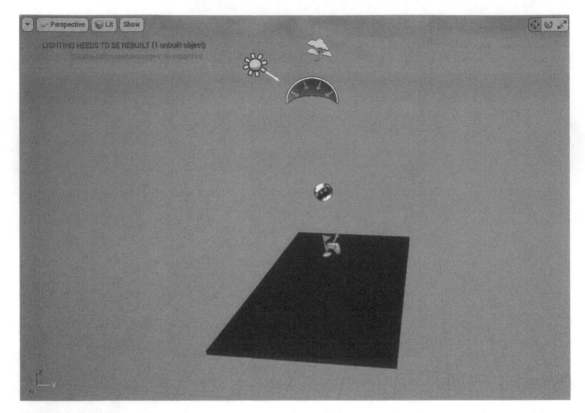

Figure 5-9. *Scene so far*

When you drag your assets now, you notice that the mesh snaps to the grid floor by the number of UU (Unreal Units, which are equal to 1 cm). You can change this default snapping value by clicking the Grid Snap Value option located in the top-right corner of the viewport (see Figure 5-10). Grid snapping is very important because it allows you to accurately place your assets where you want them.

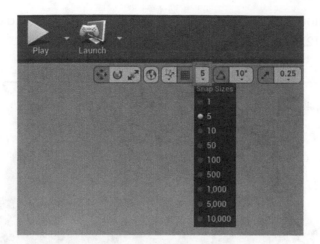

Figure 5-10. *Grid snap value option*

With this feature, you can easily move the modular assets around and place them exactly as you want.

Next, let's duplicate our floor by pressing and holding the Alt key and dragging the floor along any axis. Place the duplicated floor as shown in Figure 5-11.

Figure 5-11. *Placing a duplicated floor*

Using that method, you can duplicate the floor multiple times and create a scene similar to Figure 5-12.

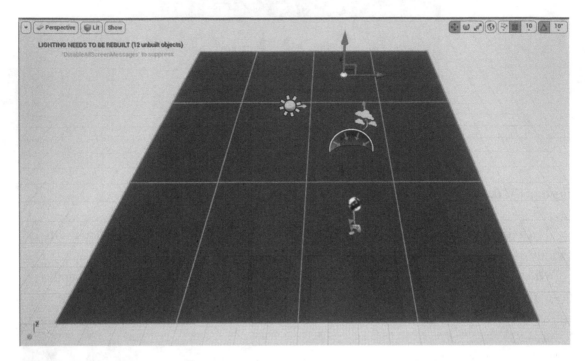

Figure 5-12. *Creating a floor setup*

Next, drag and drop the Wall_Low and Wall_Short_Side assets and set them up as shown in Figure 5-13.

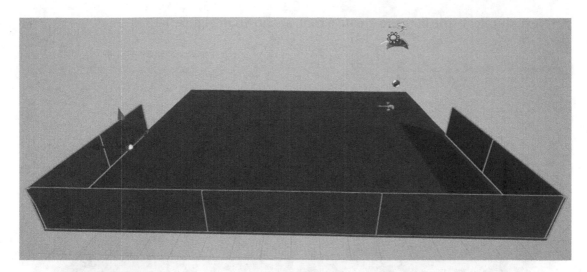

Figure 5-13. *Wall setup*

Next, drag and drop the Wall_Tall and Wall_Tall_Side assets and set them up as shown in Figure 5-14.

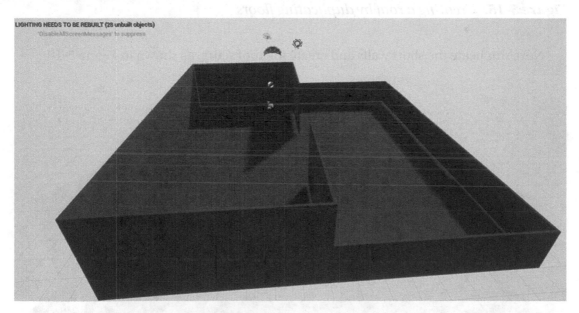

Figure 5-14. *Setup for the tall walls*

Next, duplicate the floors to create a roof, as shown in Figure 5-15.

Figure 5-15. *Creating a roof by duplicating floors*

Next, duplicate the short walls and create the roof setup, as shown in Figure 5-16.

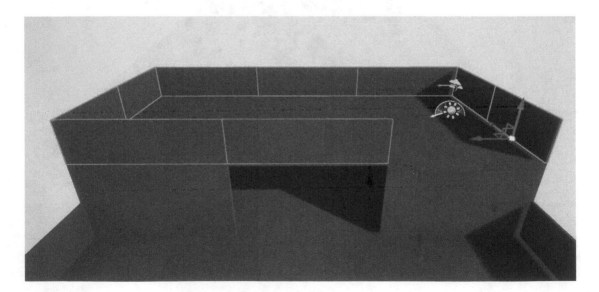

Figure 5-16. *Scene so far*

This scene can be changed according to your wishes. As you can see, all the pieces are modular, and you can easily repurpose them as you want. That is the purpose of the white-box level: flexibility is the key component.

With the basic layout done, place the Stairs and Wall_Stairs assets as shown in Figure 5-17. You can position the stairs to a value of 660 UU in the Y axis to place it exactly as it appears in the image.

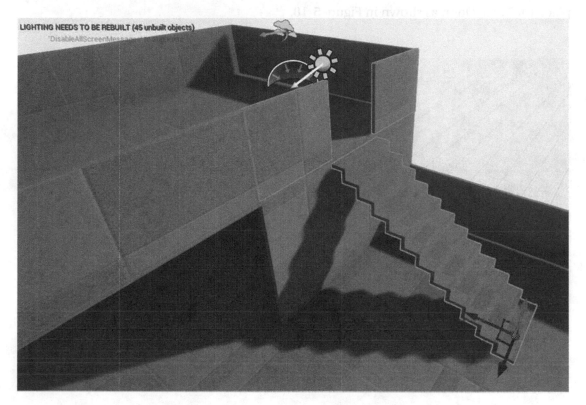

Figure 5-17. *Scene so far*

This is a very basic level layout. It can be easily changed any time before you start populating the scene with detail assets.

Adding Details

Now, let's add some assets to block out the detailed appearance of our scene. First, let's place the Wall_Door, as shown in Figure 5-18.

Figure 5-18. *Placing the Wall_Door asset*

Next, place the Sofa assets, as shown in Figure 5-19.

Figure 5-19. *Placing the sofas*

Now, let's place the plant pots, as shown in Figure 5-20.

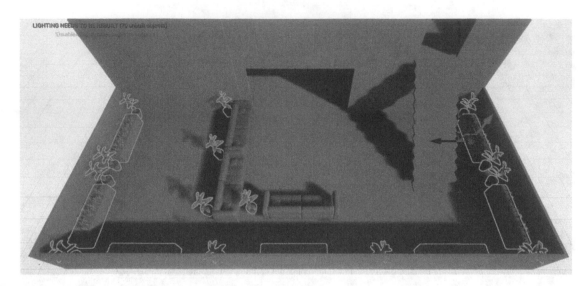

Figure 5-20. *Placing plant and grass pots*

Finally, let's place the metal rail, as shown in Figure 5-21.

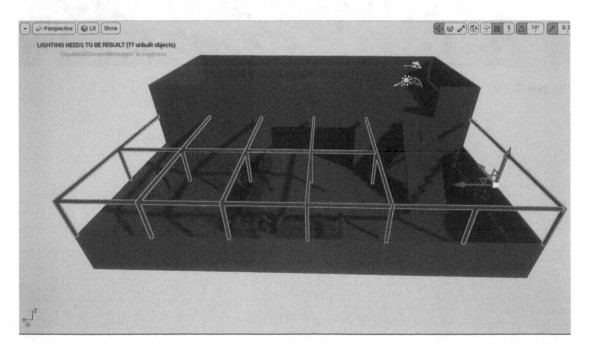

Figure 5-21. *Placing rail assets*

Press Alt+P to play and explore your level in First Person mode. You may experience some problems navigating around the environment because there are some incorrect collisions on certain meshes, like Wall_Door, Stairs, and Wall_Stairs. To fix this, double-click the asset you want to correct in the Content Browser. A new asset details window opens. In the Properties tab, scroll down until you see the Collisions option. Click the drop-down menu, select Use Complex Collision As Simple, and save (see Figure 5-22).

Note that complex collision is only good if you are working on a very small scene or an architectural vizualization scene. It is never used in a game environment because it uses a lot of memory. Complex collision calculates the collision for each vertex in the mesh. A complex model with lots of vertices easily hogs up memory and makes scenes unoptimized, so use complex collision sparingly, even in personal projects.

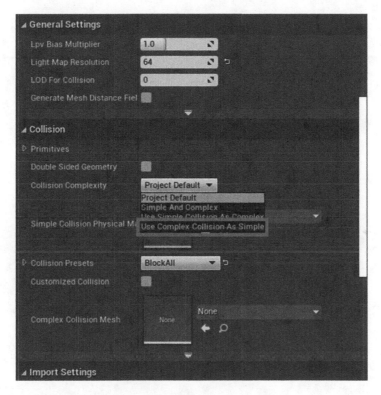

Figure 5-22. *Modifying collision setting for asset*

Now that you are done blocking out of the level, you can adjust the level layout the way that you want. It is a good practice to create something on your own based on what you have learned so far. In the next chapter, you unwrap our 3D assets.

CHAPTER 6

Creating UVs

In this chapter, you learn how to unwrap your assets and prepare them for texturing. Unwrapping is a vital step in 3D asset creation. In the unwrapping process, you layout the surface of the 3D model in a 3D format so that you can paint on it, apply bitmap textures, or procedurally texture it. Without unwrapping, it is usually not possible to texture assets properly.

When unwrapping, you need to keep the UV islands as flat as possible to reduce distortion on the applied texture. You should also keep the UV islands as even and as close to their original size as possible to ensure that you don't give too much UV space to tiny assets. Likewise, make sure to give the larger assets as much UV space as possible.

Unwrapping the Headset Asset

Let's begin by deleting the history. Go to Edit ➤ Delete All by Type ➤ History (see Figure 6-1).

© Abhishek Kumar 2021
A. Kumar, *Immersive 3D Design Visualization*, https://doi.org/10.1007/978-1-4842-6597-0_6

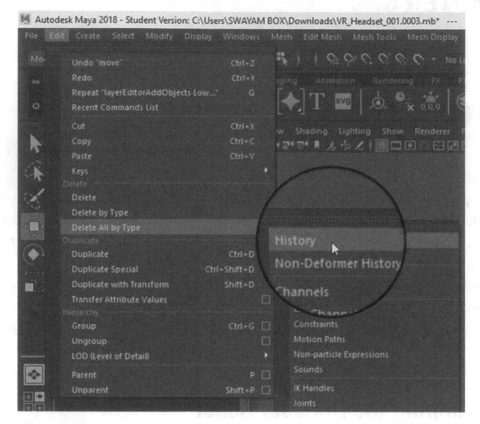

Figure 6-1. *Deleting the edit history of an object*

Next, click the quad view icon (see Figure 6-2) to split your screen into four viewports.

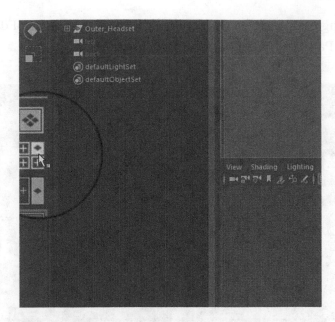

Figure 6-2. *Splitting viewport to quad mode*

Now hold the center of the quad viewport and drag it down to only have two viewports (see Figure 6-3).

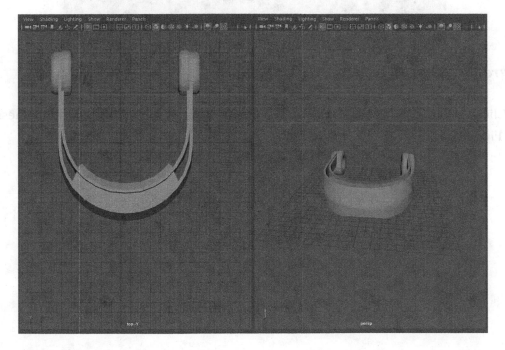

Figure 6-3. *Adjusting the viewport*

137

Next, let's change one of the panels (preferably the left one) to UV Editor mode by going to Panels ➤ Panel ➤ UV Editor (see Figure 6-4).

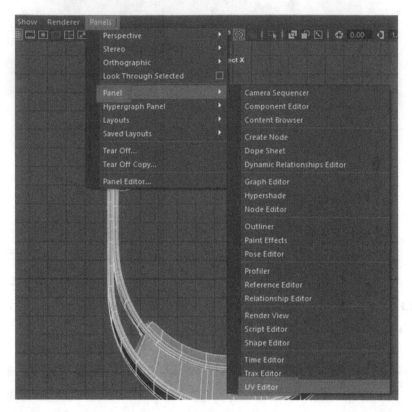

Figure 6-4. *Switching a panel to UV Editor*

Click the object to view its UVs. You see that the UVs are currently a complete mess (see Figure 6-5).

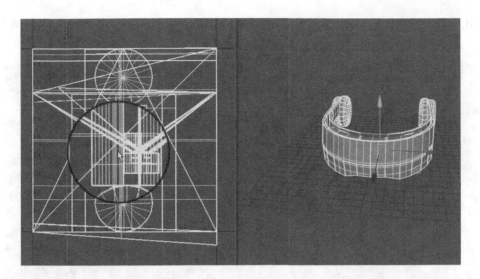

Figure 6-5. *The current state of the asset UVs*

Let's fix this by creating a proper UV layout. Click the UV tab in the menu bar at the top and then click the blue-dotted region to detach the panel to become a separate floating window (see Figure 6-6).

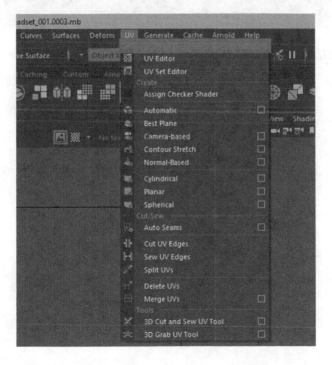

Figure 6-6. *Separating UV menu into a separate window*

139

Next, select the entire circular region of the front headset, as shown in Figure 6-7.

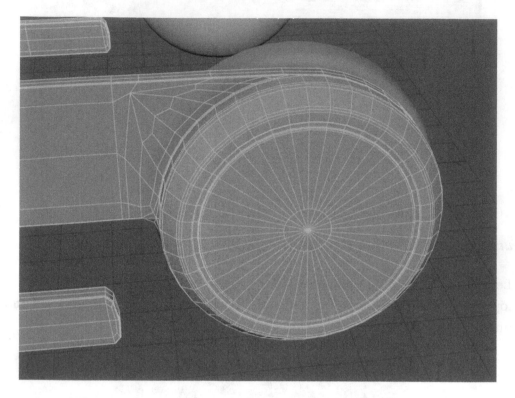

Figure 6-7. *Selecting the circular region of the front headset*

Click the Planar option in the floating UV panel window (see Figure 6-8).

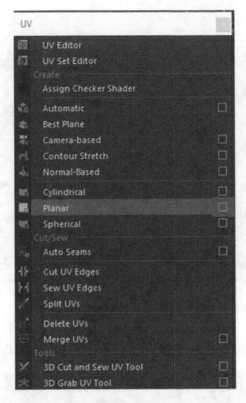

Figure 6-8. *Applying a planar map to our asset*

In the Planar Mapping Options window, select the correct axis (in our case, the X axis works), and click Apply (see Figure 6-9).

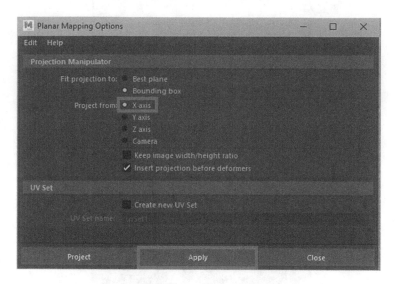

Figure 6-9. *Applying projection axis to planner mapping*

Once the UV is laid out, drag it away from the pile of other UVs (see Figure 6-10).

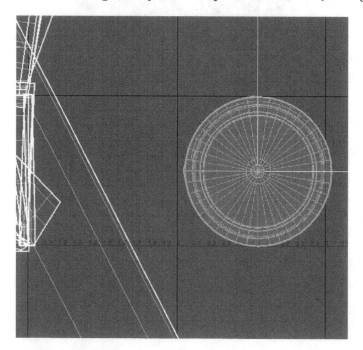

Figure 6-10. *Isolating the UV shell*

Next, select the front region, as shown in Figure 6-11.

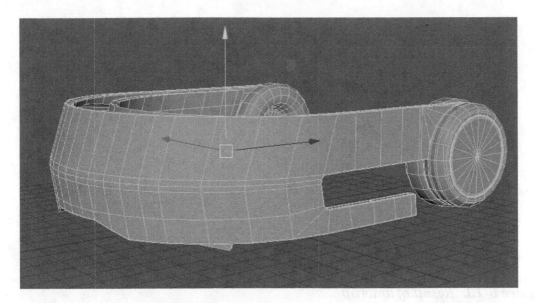

Figure 6-11. *Selecting the front piece*

Next, apply a Normal Based unwrap method to unwrap this region. Then drag it t
away from other UVs (see Figure 6-12).

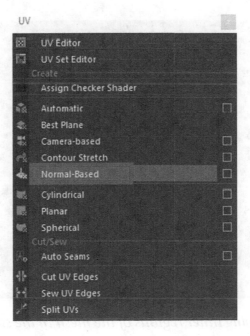

Figure 6-12. *Normal-based unwrapping*

143

Your results should look similar to Figure 6-13.

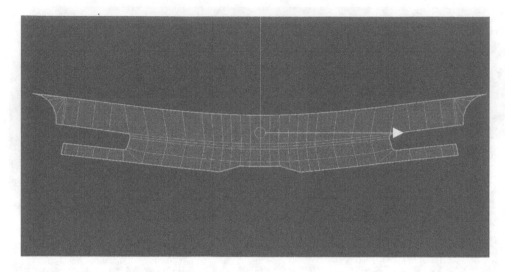

Figure 6-13.   *Result of unwrap*

Let's move a little faster. Isolate the front headset piece by pressing Shift+I while it is selected.

Next, use Normal Based unwrapping for the mesh's inner regions (see Figure 6-14).

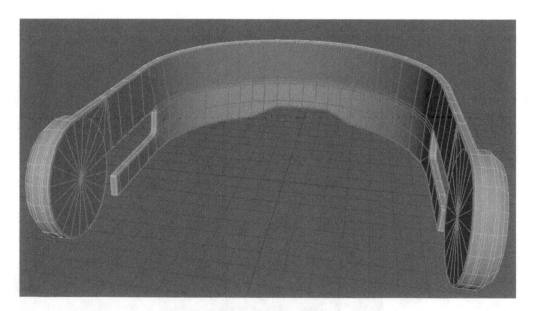

Figure 6-14.   *Unwrapping inner regions of the mesh in the same way*

Now select the top region highlighted in Figure 6-15 and apply a Planer projection from the Y axis.

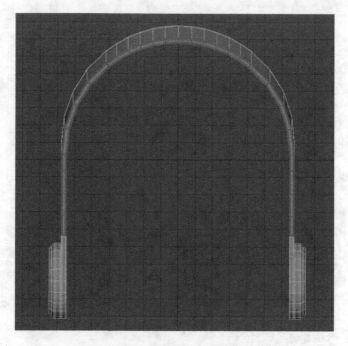

Figure 6-15. *Select this region and apply Planer from the Y axis*

Your result should look similar to Figure 6-16.

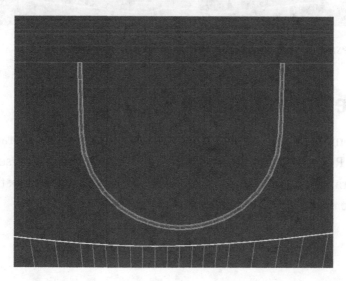

Figure 6-16. *Result of unwrap*

Figure 6-17 shows the outcome of the unwrapping.

Figure 6-17. *Result of the complete UV unwrapping process*

Testing the Unwrapping

Let's finally do some tests with a checker map to see whether your unwrap has any problems or not. Right-click your mesh, go to Apply New Material, and select Lambert. Your material parameters should be visible in the Attribute Editor. Click the small checkered square next to Color (see Figure 6-18).

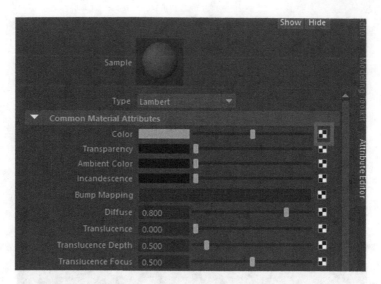

Figure 6-18. *Click the highlighted icon*

In the Create Render Node window, select Checker (see Figure 6-19).

Figure 6-19. *Applying the checker node*

The Place2DTexture settings now appear in the Attribute Editor. Here, increase RepeatUV to 40 in both parameter boxes (see Figure 6-20).

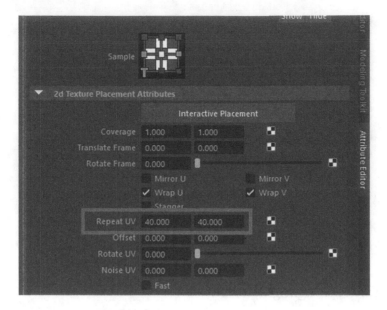

Figure 6-20. *Increasing UV tiling*

Your model should look like Figure 6-21.

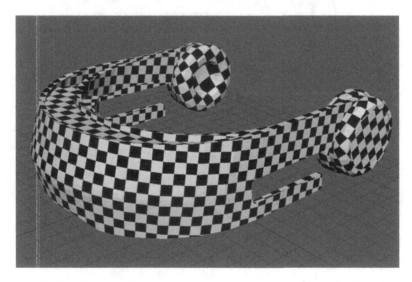

Figure 6-21. *UV checker result*

Ideally, you want to the checkers to be shaped as perfect squares. In certain regions, however, a little distortion can't be avoided. Figure 6-22 shows the results.

Figure 6-22. *Final result*

That's how you unwrap your model. This was a work of patience since everything had to be done manually, piece by piece.

That ends this chapter. In the next chapter, you study lightmaps in UE4.

CHAPTER 7

Lightmap Analysis and Correction

This chapter analyzes lightmaps and their importance. First, let's apply some placeholder materials to the scene that you created in UE4. Then, go to the Content folder ➤ StarterContent ➤ Materials and drag and drop the M_AssetPlatform material into all the meshes in your scene (see Figure 7-1).

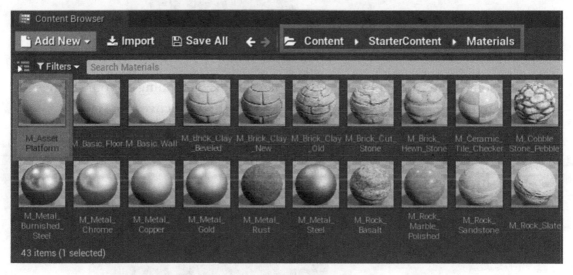

Figure 7-1. *Applying custom material to our mesh*

© Abhishek Kumar 2021
A. Kumar, *Immersive 3D Design Visualization*, https://doi.org/10.1007/978-1-4842-6597-0_7

Lightmap Analysis

Now you are ready to bake lights and see what happens. Click the drop-down arrow next to Build and select Build Lighting Only (see Figure 7-2).

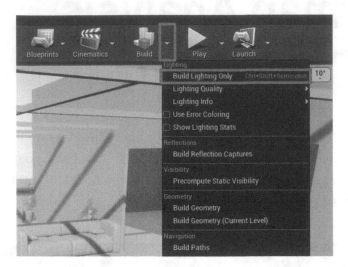

Figure 7-2. *Building lights only*

Give it some time. The light building can take a while, depending on your settings. You can go to Lighting Quality and see which quality setting is active (see Figure 7-3).

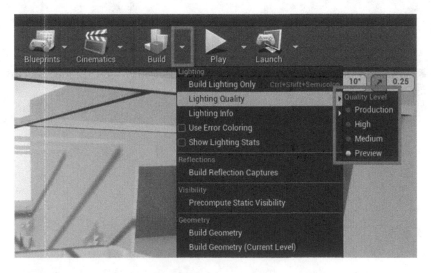

Figure 7-3. *Setting lighting quality level*

CHAPTER 7 LIGHTMAP ANALYSIS AND CORRECTION

Preview quality bakes the fastest, but it is the lowest quality. Production takes the longest time to bake, but the lighting quality is the highest. In this case, you can set the lighting quality to Medium or Preview quality. Once baking is finished, you should see a similar result to Figure 7-4.

Figure 7-4. *Lighting build result*

The result in Figure 7-4 may look slightly yellowish. You can produce a similar result by increasing the light intensity to a high number, in our case 15, by enabling Temperature in the Details panel. Then, decrease the temperature value to 4000 (see Figure 7-5).

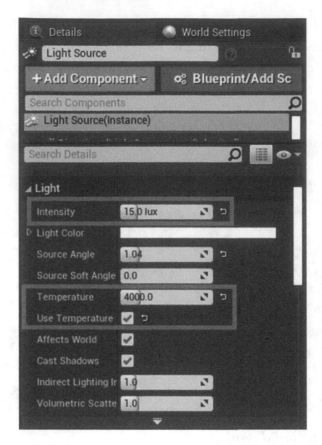

Figure 7-5. *Light settings*

Now let's come back to the result of the light bake. As you can see, our bake has many problems, including low resolution for the shadows and sharp transitions. To fix this, you need to create lightmap UVs.

Double-click the Wall_Tall asset in the Content Browser to open the window that gives detailed information about that asset (see Figure 7-6).

Figure 7-6. *Asset details window*

You can click the UV drop-down menu to view the UVs present in your mesh. UV Channel 0 is the map created in Maya. UV Channel 1 is a lightmap UV that UE4 generated automatically (see Figure 7-7).

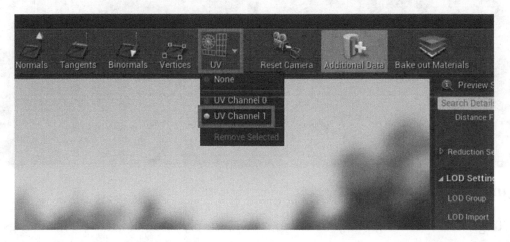

Figure 7-7. *Viewing UV channels*

And as you can see in Figure 7-8, the automatic lightmap UV generated by UE4 is displayed.

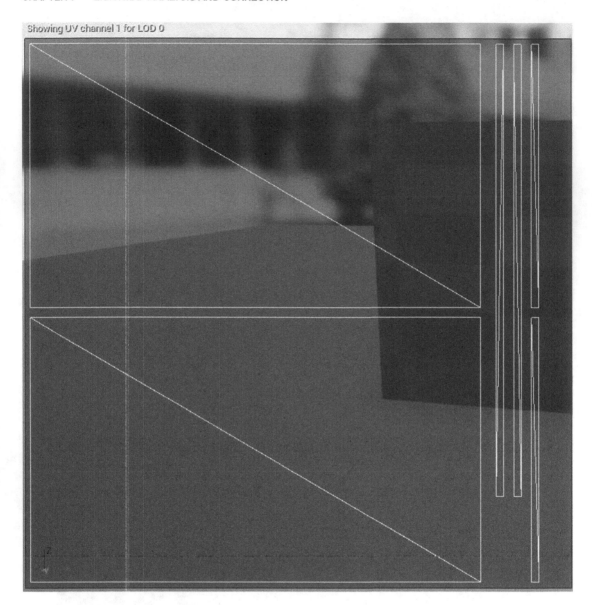

Figure 7-8. *Lightmap UV*

To generate some lightmap UVs of your own, simply scroll down to Build Settings and set the Destination Lightmap Index channel number. In our case, it is channel 1, although you can select what you want, and then click Apply Changes (see Figure 7-9).

This generates new lightmap UVs based on the UV map that you created. It uses a flawed algorithm that does not always produce good results, but you can sometimes use it to create lightmap UVs for small and simple assets.

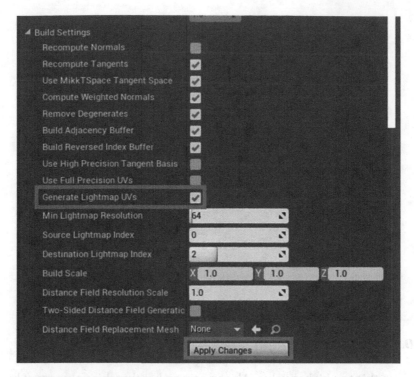

Figure 7-9. *Generating lightmaps*

Once you click Apply Changes, a new channel is created if you entered a number larger than the number of available channels in your mesh. And a new lightmap is regenerated.

Next, let's increase lightmap's resolution to store higher-resolution shadow information and various other kinds of light information. To do this, scroll down and locate Light Map Resolution under General Settings (see Figure 7-10).

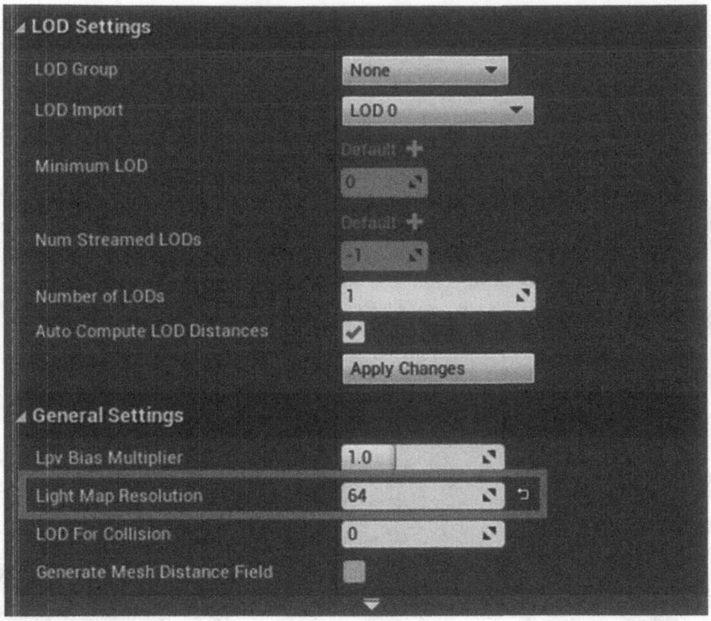

Figure 7-10.   Light map resolution

Let's increase this to a higher value. Always remember that this value must be in powers of 2, meaning the value has to be 2, 4, 8, 16, 32, 64, 128, 256, 512, 1024, or 2048, and so on. Since this wall is large, let's increase the value to 1024. Remember, the higher the lightmap value, the more memory it uses. Don't use a high-resolution lightmap on everything.

Once done, click Save (see Figure 7-11).

Figure 7-11.   Saving changes

With that done, let's rebake our lights and see the result. As you can see in Figure 7-12, the walls that you edited are already significantly improved.

Figure 7-12. *The edited walls show better results after light bake*

Using Lightmass Importance Volume

Before you do the final baking, let's bring in a very important volume that tells UE4 where to focus the light calculation in the world. UE4 does not automatically know how you set up your level and where you want to focus the lighting. Lightmass Importance Volume serves this purpose. In the Place Actors panel, click Volumes, and you see it in the list (see Figure 7-13).

Figure 7-13. *Lightmass Importance Volume*

Drag and drop Lightmass Importance Volume into your scene. It is small at first. Use the Scale tool (shortcut R) and scale it large enough to completely surround the entire scene and contain it inside itself (see Figure 7-14).

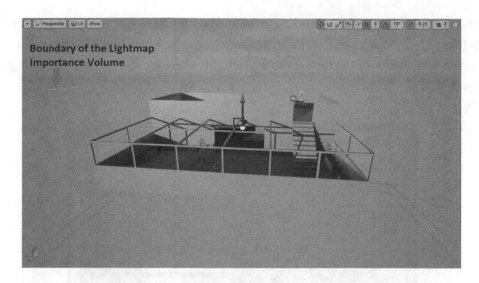

Figure 7-14. *The boundary of Lightmass Importance Volume in light yellow color*

Eliminating Baking Errors

It's time to tweak a few settings in the light to eliminate some baking errors. Go to the Windows tab in the menu bar and click World Settings (see Figure 7-15). This opens a World Settings panel next to your Details panel.

Figure 7-15. *World Settings*

In the World Settings panel, under the Lightmass tab, you need to change a few settings (see Figure 7-16). First, reduce the Static Lighting Level Scale to 0.4. Then, increase the Indirect Lighting Quality to 3.0. Finally, increase the Num Indirect Lighting Bounces to 7.

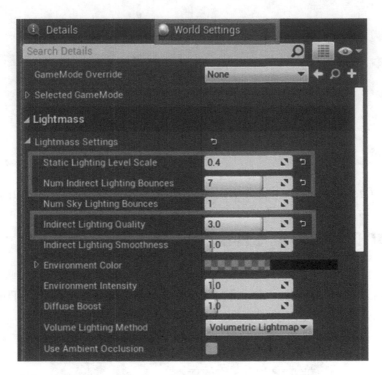

Figure 7-16. *Lightmass Settings*

Next, increase the Num Sky Lighting Bounces to 5 and Indirect Lighting Smoothness to 1.2 (see Figure 7-17).

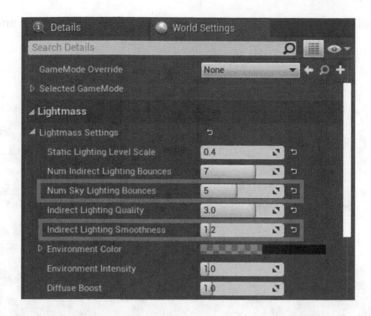

Figure 7-17. *Changing more Lightmass settings*

Baking the Scene

You are ready to bake the scene. Switch the Lighting Quality to Production, and click Bake (see Figure 7-18).

Figure 7-18. *Increase Lighting Quality*

The results of the completed baking are shown in Figures 7-19, 7-20, and 7-21.

Figure 7-19. *Result of bake 1*

Figure 7-20. *Result of bake 2*

Figure 7-21. *Result of bake 3*

Tweak the lightmap settings for all the other assets, and you can achieve good results. In the next chapter, you learn about PBR Integrated Texturing workflows.

CHAPTER 8

PBR Integrated Texturing

In this chapter, you see PBR integrated texturing workflows. There are multiple tools available to aid in texturing your assets. Throughout this chapter, Quixel Megascans and Substance Painter are used. Let's start with a short introduction to both software applications.

Substance Painter

Substance Painter is an industry-standard texturing tool used by both AAA and indie studios. It is very user-friendly and easy to use. A large community constantly offers free assets that you can use for your projects. A premium asset library called Substance Source provides a high-quality and curated library of assets that you can access if you subscribe to Substance Suite.

Let's look at Substance Painter's basic controls and interface. This book uses version 2019.3.2. When you first launch Substance Painter, your window looks similar to Figure 8-1.

© Abhishek Kumar 2021
A. Kumar, *Immersive 3D Design Visualization*, https://doi.org/10.1007/978-1-4842-6597-0_8

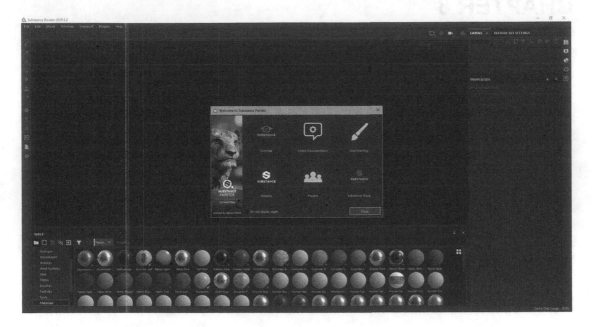

Figure 8-1. *Substance Painter interface*

At the bottom of the screen is the *shelf*, which allows you to access various assets that you need during the texturing process. The Properties window is where you change and tweak your layers, brushes, materials, and so on. The Layer panel allows you to add, edit, and manage layers. Substance Painter is a layer-based texturing program; therefore, you work with layers a lot. The Texture Set Settings panel allows you to manage attributes related to texture sets.

Now let's discuss Substance Painter's controls. Press Alt+Left-click to rotate the view. Press Alt+Middle-click to pan the view. Press Alt+Right-click to zoom the view. Table 8-1 lists many of the hotkeys and their purposes.

Table 8-1. *Substance Painter Hotkeys*

Hotkey	Effect
Alt+LMB	Rotate view
Alt+MMB	Pan view
Alt+RMB	Zoom view
Alt+Shift+LMB	Rotate camera while snapping
F	The center camera on mesh
F5	Switch to perspective camera
F6	Switch to orthographic camera
LMB	Paint/Use tool
]	Increase tool size
[	Decrease tool size
F9	Painting mode
F10	Rendering mode
Shift+LMB	Draw straight line
Ctrl+Shift+LMB	Draw straight line while snapping
B	Switch mesh map being displayed
M	Material mode
C	Switch channel displayed

Quixel Megascans

Let's now look at Quixel Megascans—specifically, Quixel Bridge. Quixel Bridge is software that allows you to seamlessly integrate Quixel Megascans with other DCC applications in just a few clicks. Figure 8-2 shows the Quixel Bridge interface.

Figure 8-2. *Quixel Bridge*

Quixel Megascans is free to Unreal Engine 4 users. You can access the entire library of more than 12,000 3D scanned assets, including textures and 3D meshes. Click an asset in Quixel Bridge to download and store it on your hard drive. Once an asset is downloaded, you can export it to any DCC application you choose (see Figure 8-3).

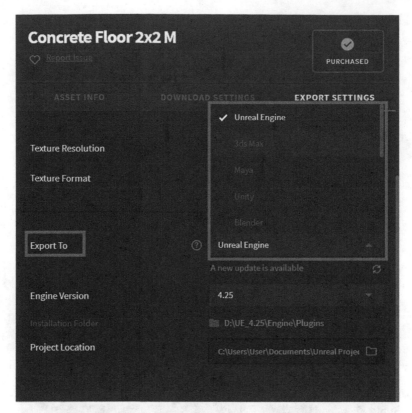

Figure 8-3. *Quixel Bridge export settings*

For every application that you export to, there is a plugin that aids in this exchange process. When you select a DCC application from the list, you are given the option to download and install the related plugin, as shown in Figure 8-4.

Once the plugin has been downloaded and installed, you are good to go.

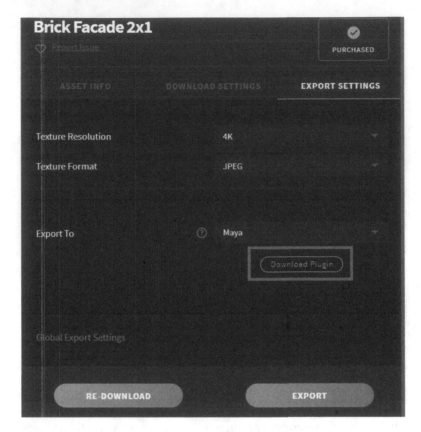

Figure 8-4. *Downloading plugin for DCC of choice*

This project uses Unreal Engine 4 and its plugins. First, download the UE4 plugin. Next, set the Engine Version to the one you are using. Then, set the Installation Folder the same as the UE4 installation directory. The Project Location is the same folder in which you have saved your project (see Figure 8-5). Make sure to keep UE4 running when exporting assets; otherwise, it gives an error message. The UE4 should be running, and the Livelink should be installed and active before you export assets to UE4.

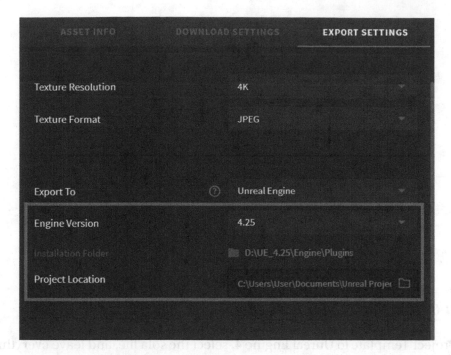

Figure 8-5. *Setting up a plugin for UE4*

PBR Texturing

Let's start texturing some of our assets. We will begin with Substance Painter. First, you need to import an asset—the sofa asset for this purpose. Launch Substance Painter and click File ➤ New Project (see Figure 8-6).

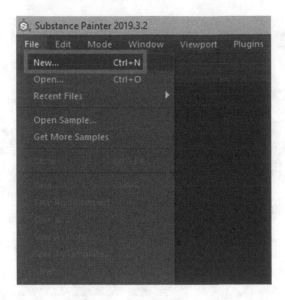

Figure 8-6. *Creating a new project*

Set Project Template to Unreal Engine 4, select the sofa file, and leave everything else at the default. Next, click OK to create a project (see Figure 8-7). Make sure that Import Cameras is not checked because you are not importing cameras for this project.

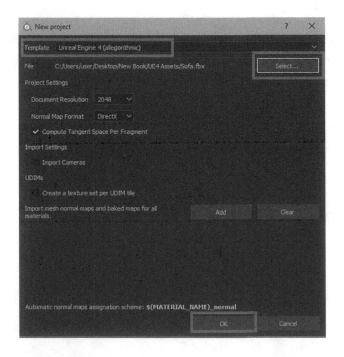

Figure 8-7. *New project settings*

The sofa should be in the center of the screen. And now you are ready to bake the mesh maps. Go to Texture Set Settings and click Bake Mesh Maps (see Figure 8-8). Your screen is split into two when you open Substance Painter for the first time. You can press F1, F2, or F3 to switch between modes, which are the Split layout, 3D-only layout, and 2D-only layout, respectively. Press F2 to switch to 3D-only view mode.

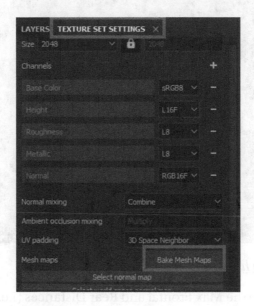

Figure 8-8. *Baking mesh maps*

The Baking window opens, allowing you to change several properties related to mesh map baking. First, disable the ID channel because there aren't any ID maps for our mesh. Next, add the high poly mesh by clicking the add-file icon next to the High Definition Meshes option (see Figure 8-9).

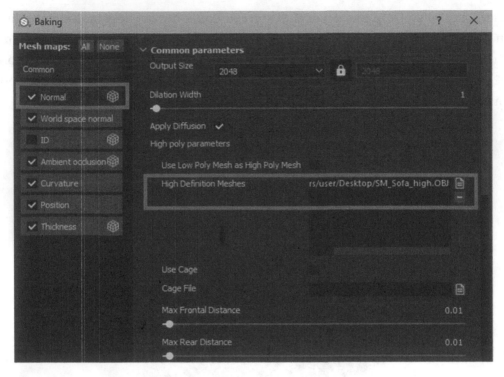

Figure 8-9. *Importing high poly mesh*

Let's slightly increase the Max Frontal and Rear Distances (i.e., by 0.03 and 0.05, respectively). This increases the ray casting distance by a small amount and helps with baking. This number is usually hard to determine; trying out a small value to see what works can be helpful.

An option called Average Normals is enabled by default. If your mesh has hard normals, then it is beneficial to enable it so that Substance Painter averages the normals between the high poly and low poly maps, ensuring a smoother result. Although you may disable this if the hard normals need to be preserved for some reason. Since both high poly and low poly meshes have smoothed normals, you can disable it. But you should keep it enabled if you want smooth normals across the mesh; it won't make much difference. With that, your settings should look similar to Figure 8-10.

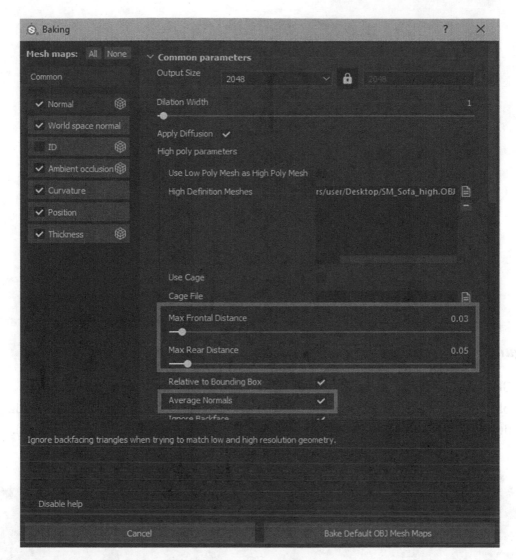

Figure 8-10. *Bake settings*

Next, scroll down and change the Match setting to By Mesh Name, as shown in Figure 8-11.

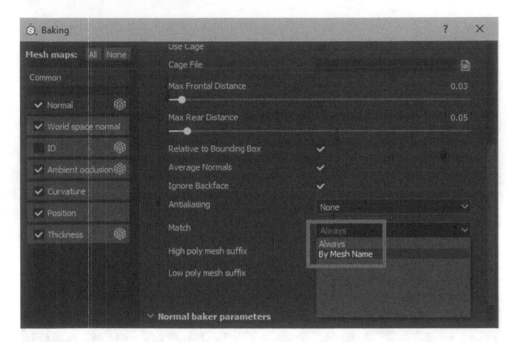

Figure 8-11. *Match by mesh name*

Go to Ambient Occlusion and set Self Occlusion to By Same Mesh Name. Next, disable Thickness because you won't need this map. Then, click Bake. Once the baking has finished, you see the normal map details baked into your mesh (see Figure 8-12).

Figure 8-12. *Normal information baked into the mesh*

Texturing

Now let's texture the sofa. Drag and drop Fabric Rough Aligned onto your Layer Stack. You should see something similar to Figure 8-13.

Figure 8-13. *Fabric Rough Aligned*

Your mesh should look like Figure 8-14.

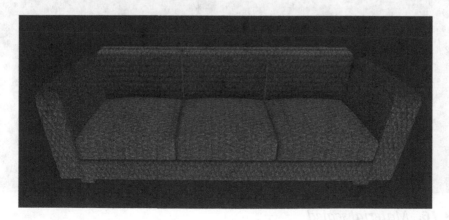

Figure 8-14. *Fabric applied to the mesh*

Next, go to the Properties window and in the Projection menu, select Tri-planar, which ensures that your UV seams are hidden (see Figure 8-15).

Figure 8-15. *Tri-planar projection*

Next, under UV transformations, increase Scale to 4. Your result should look similar to Figure 8-16.

Figure 8-16. *Material scaled*

Next, under Parameters, change the color to dark blue (see Figure 8-17).

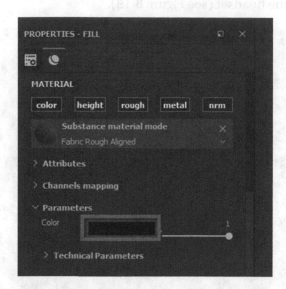

Figure 8-17. *Changing material color*

Your result should look similar to Figure 8-18.

Figure 8-18. *Final sofa*

The sofa is ready to export to UE4.

Next, let's texture the headset (see Figure 8-19).

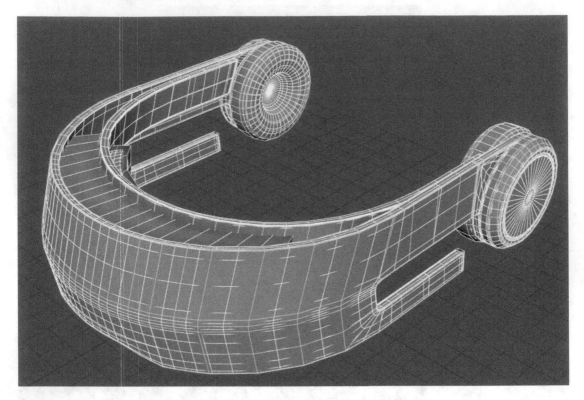

Figure 8-19. *Overlapping High poly and low poly models*

Select the low poly model, go to File ➤ Export, and select Obj exporter. Export to where it is convenient using the name Headset_low. Export the high poly model in the same way, but use the name Headset_high. After that, open Substance Painter.

Import the headset model the same way you imported the sofa model. Once done, go to Bake using similar settings as the sofa, but this time, import the Headset_high model as the high poly mesh (see Figure 8-20) and leave Match at the default settings (i.e., do not set as By Mesh Name).

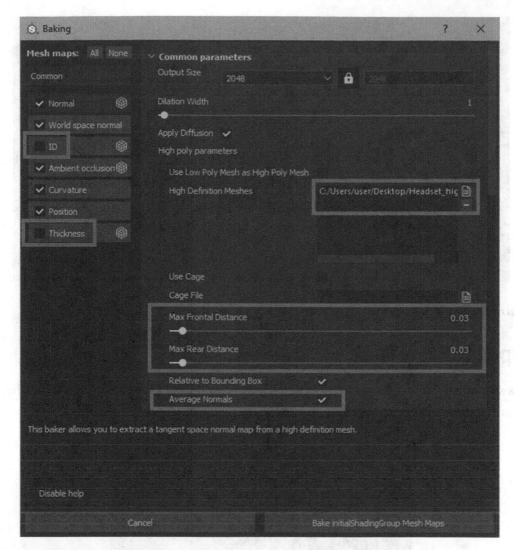

Figure 8-20. *Baking settings*

With that done, you should see the details baked into your mesh.
Your result should look something like Figure 8-21.

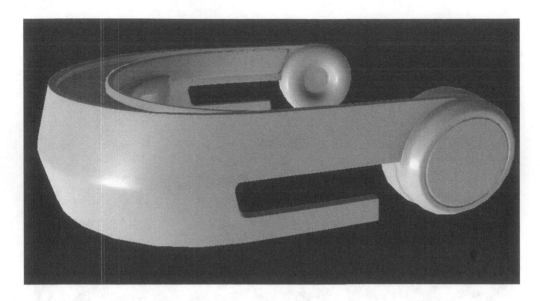

Figure 8-21. *Bake results*

Applying Materials

Let's start applying some materials by adding Plastic Matte Pure material from the shelf to our mesh (see Figure 8-22).

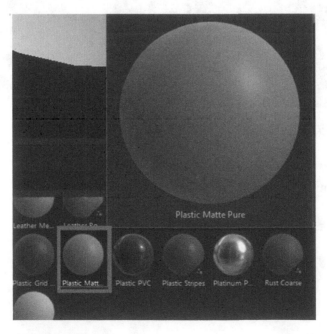

Figure 8-22. *Plastic Matte Pure*

Next, go to Material Properties and change the settings as shown in Figure 8-23.

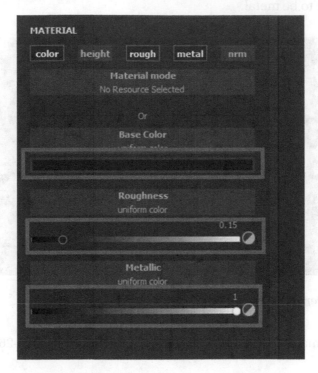

Figure 8-23. *Material settings*

Double-click Plastic Material in the Layer Stack and rename it Metal_Default (see Figure 8-24). This is optional.

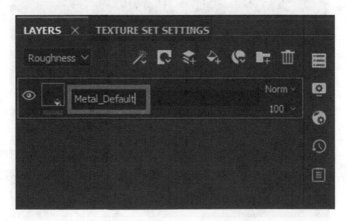

Figure 8-24. *Renaming our material*

Figure 8-25 shows that the entire mesh picked up the material—even those places that you don't want to be metal.

Figure 8-25. *Material covering the whole mesh*

Right-click the material and select Add Black Mask (see Figure 8-26).

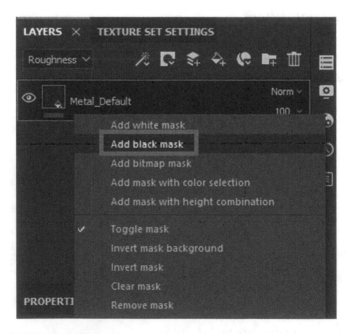

Figure 8-26. *Add black mask*

You see that the entire model has become untextured. Make sure the mask is selected, and then click Polygon Fill and then Mesh Fill. Also, make sure the fill color is set to white (see Figure 8-27).

Figure 8-27. *Fill settings*

Click the parts that you want to be metal. The metal material fills those parts of the mesh (see Figure 8-28).

Figure 8-28. *Filling metal color*

Next, try filling the white, untextured regions of the mesh with a Fabric material. First, add a Fabric material of your choice (in our case, it is the Knitted Sweater material with a dark color) and then apply a black mask to the material. Using the fill settings shown in Figure 8-27, click the untextured regions. Your results should look similar to Figure 8-29.

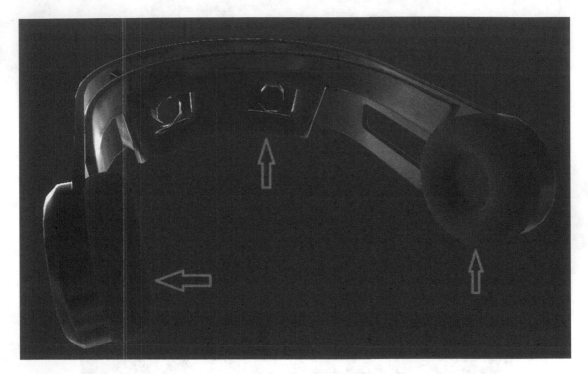

Figure 8-29. Fabric material applied to parts of the mesh

As you can see, the mesh is way too clean. Let's add some roughness variation to it—specifically, to the metal parts. First, right-click your metal material and select Duplicate. Next, right-click the mask of the duplicated material and select Clear Mask. Finally, right-click the now clear mask of the duplicated metal material and select Add Generator (see Figure 8-30).

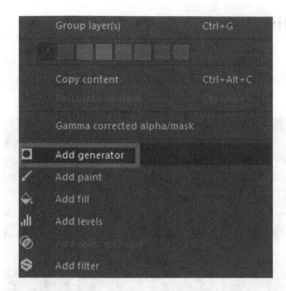

Figure 8-30. *Add generator*

Next, click Generator and select the Dirt generator (see Figure 8-31).

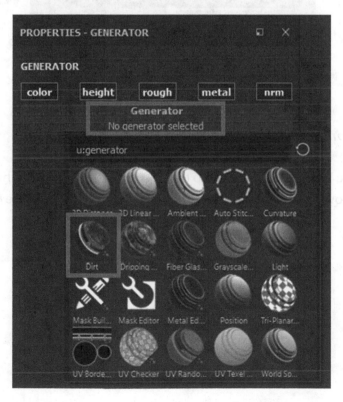

Figure 8-31. *Adding Dirt generator*

Dealing with Dirt

You now see procedural dirt being generated on your mesh. You can modify the Dirt settings in the Properties panel. Use the Dirt Level option (see Figure 8-32).

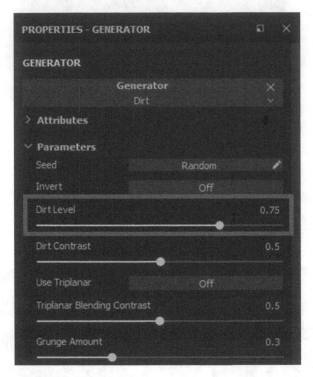

Figure 8-32.   *Controlling Dirt amount*

Next, click the Duplicated material so that its properties appear in the Properties tab. Here you scroll down and disable all channels except Rough (see Figure 8-33).

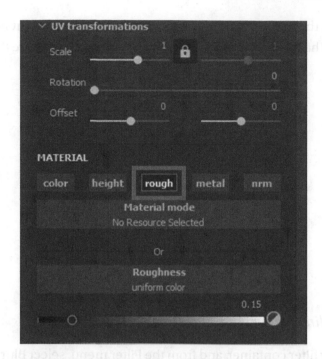

Figure 8-33. *Disable all channels except rough*

Next, increase Roughness to a value of 0.35. Your mesh should now look similar to Figure 8-34.

Figure 8-34. *Procedural dirt effect on mesh*

As you can see, the dirt effect now appears on our mesh. But right now, it is too strong. Right-click the mask and apply a filter from the list (see Figure 8-35).

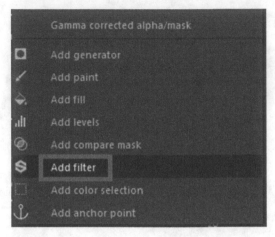

Figure 8-35. *Adding a filter*

Click the empty filter container, and from the Filter menu, select Blur (see Figure 8-36).

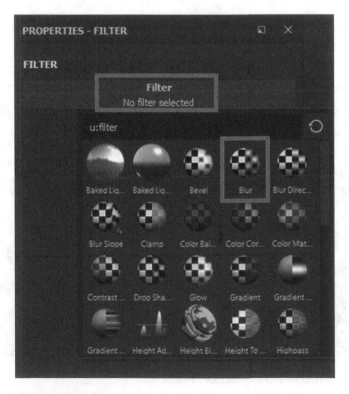

Figure 8-36. *Applying Blur filter*

Reduce Blur Intensity to 0.3 in the Properties panel (see Figure 8-37).

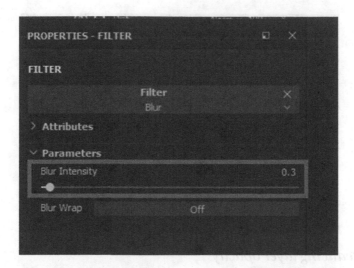

Figure 8-37. *Decreasing Blur Intensity*

If the blur effect is still too strong and visible, click the active channel drop-down menu and select Roughness (see Figure 8-38).

Figure 8-38. *Changing the active channel*

Next, reduce the opacity of the layer to a low value; in our case, 40 (see Figure 8-39).

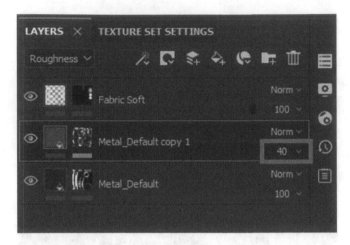

Figure 8-39. *Reducing layer opacity*

Next, create a Paint layer by clicking the button highlighted in Figure 8-40.

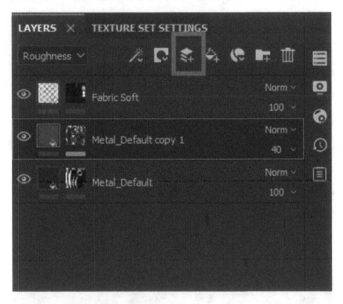

Figure 8-40. *Creating a new paint layer*

Once this layer has been created, go to its properties, and disable all channels except Normals (see Figure 8-41).

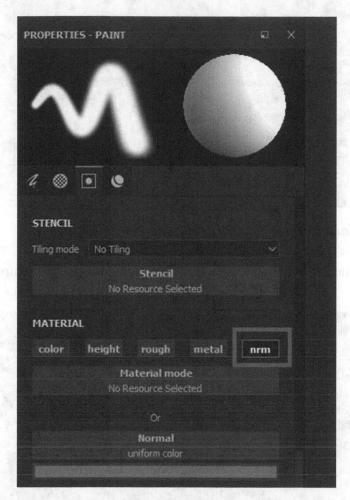

Figure 8-41. *Only Normal channel is active*

Switch to the Hard Surfaces category on the shelf and select any one normal map that you like (see Figure 8-42). I selected Vent Circles.

Figure 8-42. *Hard surfaces that ship with Substance Painter*

Drop it into the Normal map slot in the Properties window (see Figure 8-43).

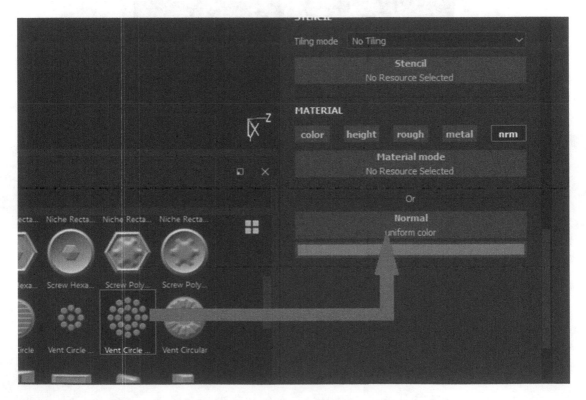

Figure 8-43. *Drag and drop Normal map into Normal map slot*

You are now ready to paint this detail. You can use the [and] keys to decrease and increase the size of the brush, respectively. Before you paint, you need to remove the alpha map from the brush. To do this, scroll up and click the X button next to the Alpha map slot (see Figure 8-44).

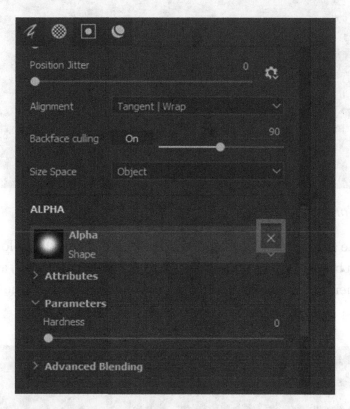

Figure 8-44. *Removing alpha map*

After that, simply click your mesh to paint the alpha map. You can drag and drop another normal map into the normal map slot to paint a different pattern at any time. My results are shown in Figure 8-45.

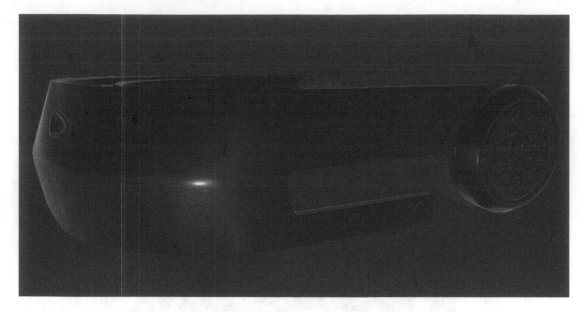

Figure 8-45. *Normal painting*

Finally, create another Paint layer, but this time, enable only the Color channel. Using the default brush, fill some color into the painted Normal details, as shown in Figure 8-46. Remember, you can hold the Shift key to draw a straight line between two clicks.

Figure 8-46. *Painting some details*

If you experience problems painting in Perspective view, you can change to Orthographic view by pressing F6. Press F5 to switch back to Perspective view. Also, you can enable Symmetry by clicking the button highlighted in Figure 8-47. Symmetry allows you to work on one side as your work is automatically carried over to the other side.

Figure 8-47. *Enabling Symmetry*

This chapter overviewed a PBR-based texturing workflow. There is more to creating realistic texturing, but that is beyond the scope of this book. Hopefully, what you have learned so far will guide you going further.

In the next chapter, you learn about material integration in UE4.

CHAPTER 9

Material Design and Integration

You have created some materials, now let's look at how to import and integrate them in UE4. In this chapter, you export materials from Substance Painter and learn how to set up the exporter for UE4. Then, you import textures into UE4 and set up master materials. After that, you use Quixel Bridge to import materials from Quixel Megascans and witness how fast and powerful Quixel Bridge can be.

Exporting from Substance Painter

Let's start by opening the file that you created in Substance Painter. Then go to File ➤ Export Textures (see Figure 9-1).

Figure 9-1. *Export textures*

A. Kumar, *Immersive 3D Design Visualization*, https://doi.org/10.1007/978-1-4842-6597-0_9

In the Export Document window, set Config to Unreal Engine 4 (Packed), as shown in Figure 9-2. This ensures that the textures are exported in a way that UE4 can properly use them.

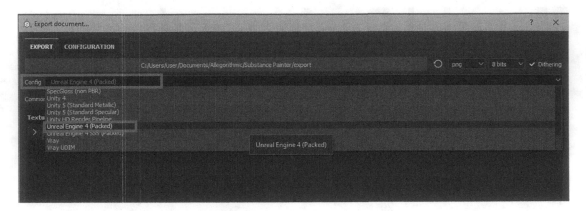

Figure 9-2. *Changing export config*

To see how the textures are set up, go to Configuration ➤ Unreal Engine 4 (Packed) (see Figure 9-3).

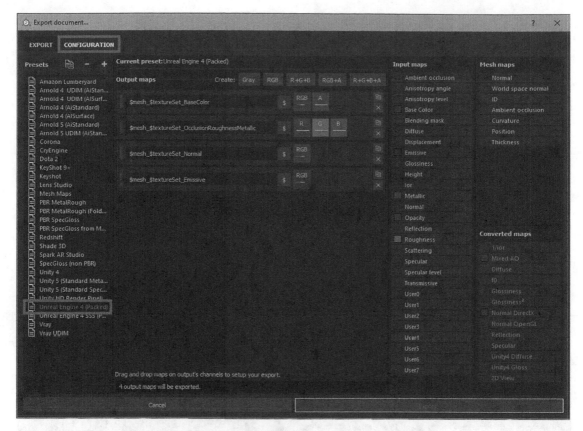

Figure 9-3. *Texture configuration for export*

In the Configuration window, under Output Maps, our texture maps are ready to be exported. Note the various settings. The map named BaseColor has one RGB (red, green, blue) input and one A input; an input map is plugged into each of them. You can see which one is plugged in based on the color in the output map and the corresponding color in the input map.

The OcclusionRoughnessMetallic map has three inputs plugged into a single output texture map. This map is sometimes referred to as the ORM (Ambient **O**cclusion, **R**oughness, **M**etallic) map for convenience. Occlusion maps, Roughness maps, and Metallic maps are grayscale. When the three different channels are plugged into a texture, you can save memory and space, and optimize your project.

These presets are set up by the Substance Painter team so that you can quickly export your texture maps and send them to the DCC application of your choice.

Let's now switch back to the Export tab and change some more settings. Increase the document resolution to 2048×2048, and set the image format to targa, as shown in Figure 9-4.

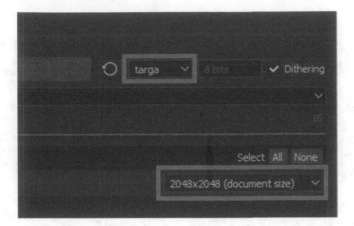

Figure 9-4. *Export settings*

Now, you are ready to export your maps. Set the export destination to the folder that you want, and then click Export (see Figure 9-5).

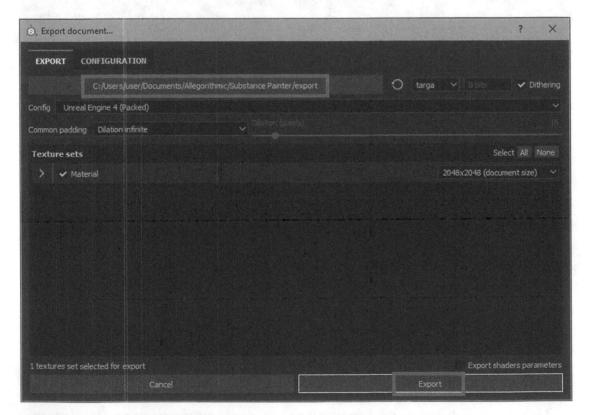

Figure 9-5. *Setting the export destination and exporting textures*

Working with Materials in UE4

Once your materials have been exported, open UE4. But before you drop these materials into UE4, use the naming convention for textures. Open the textures wherever you have saved them, and then rename them T_Sofa_BaseColor, T_Sofa_OcclusionRoughnessMetallic, and T_Sofa_Normal, respectively.

Create a folder for storing the texture maps. Name this folder Textures. Drag and drop your textures into this folder. You should see your materials in the Content Browser (see Figure 9-6).

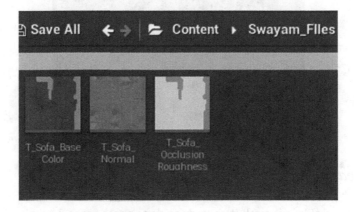

Figure 9-6. *Texture maps imported in UE4*

Now let's create a material using these texture maps. Double-click T_Sofa_ORM, and under Texture, make sure that sRGB is disabled. (UE4 should have done this automatically.) Right-click in an empty space in the Content Browser, and under Create Basic Asset, select Material (see Figure 9-7).

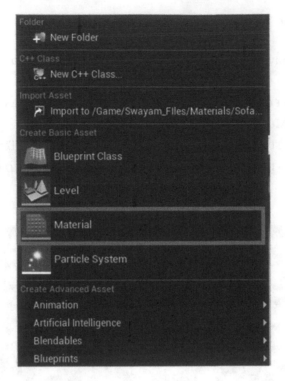

Figure 9-7. *Creating Material asset*

Name this material in a way that corresponds to your asset. I named it MM_Sofa. Next, double-click it to launch the Material Editor window. Your window should look similar to Figure 9-8. You can open the Content Browser by going to Window ➤ Content Browser ➤ Content Browser 1.

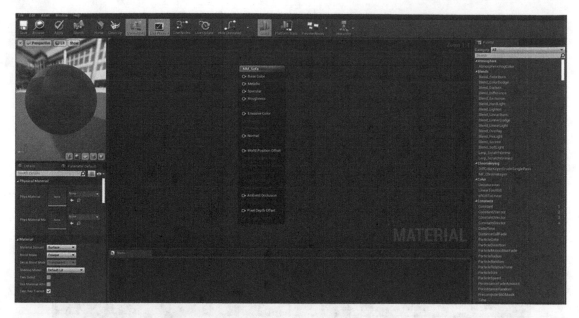

Figure 9-8. *Material Editor window*

This is a node-based Material Editor, where you use various nodes and functions to create material.

Let's begin by dragging our textures from the Content Browser and dropping them into the Material Editor window. Arrange the textures as shown in Figure 9-9. This is your introduction to the Blueprints system. You are using node-based programming to create materials. By connecting nodes, you assign different functions to your overall node tree, which, once executed, produces the material.

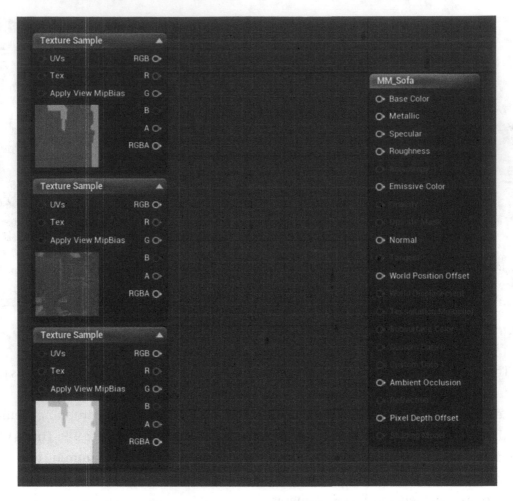

Figure 9-9. *Bringing and arranging our material in Material Editor*

Let's now add some material functions to edit our materials. Right-click in an empty space, search for CheapContrast_RGB, and add it to the editor. Next, search for Multiply and add it as well. Connect the Base Color node's RGB output pin to the CheapContrast_ RGB input pin. Next, connect the CheapContrast_RGB output to the Multiply input. Finally, connect Multiply to MM_Sofa's Base Color input. Your setup should look similar to Figure 9-10.

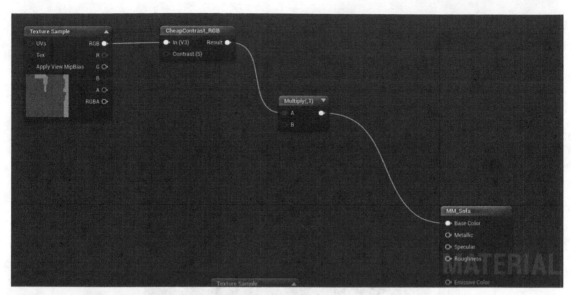

Figure 9-10. *Setup so far*

Next, press and hold thc alphanumcric 1 key on your keyboard and left-click anywhere to add a Constant node. Right-click this constant, and select Convert to Parameter (see Figure 9-11). Alternatively, you can press S and click to add a Parameter node.

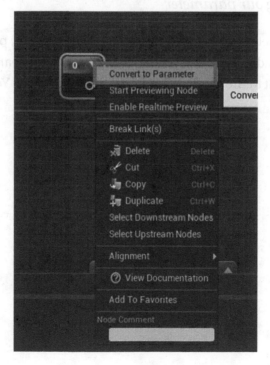

Figure 9-11. *Converting constant to parameter*

Name this parameter Contrast in the Details panel on the left (see Figure 9-12).

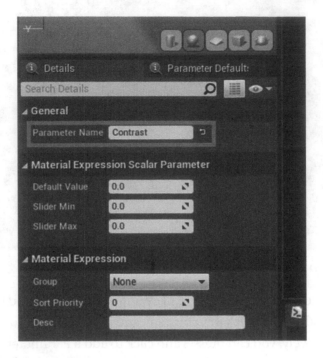

Figure 9-12. *Naming our parameter*

Connect the parameter to CheapContrast_RGB's Contrast (S) pin.

Next, right-click to add Constant3Vector, and convert it to a parameter as well. Name it Tint. Connect it to the Multiply node's bottom input pin. Your setup should look similar to Figure 9-13.

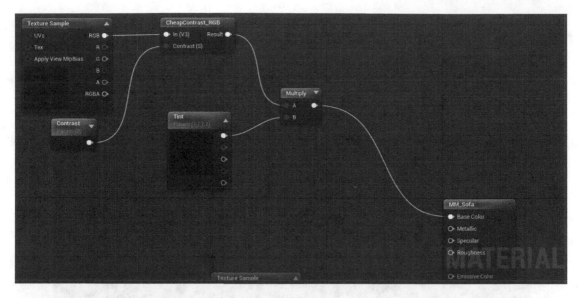

Figure 9-13. *Setup so far*

Click the Tint parameter node. In the Details panel, set its default value to be completely white (see Figure 9-14).

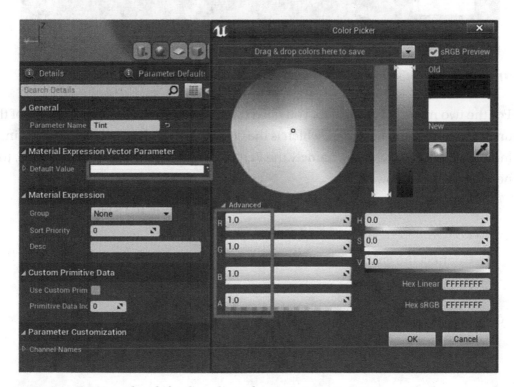

Figure 9-14. *Setting the default value of our tint parameter*

211

Connect your normal map to the main material, as shown in Figure 9-15.

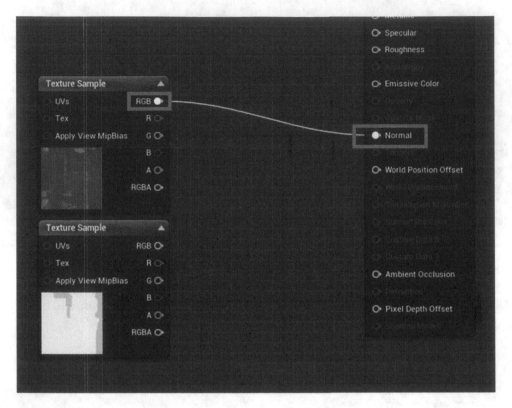

Figure 9-15.   *Connecting normal map*

For the two maps in Figure 9-15, you need the data stored in all three channels of the texture map. But for the next map, which is the ORM map, you need the data stored in the individual texture channels, namely the Red, Green, and Blue channels. For this, the connecting goes as follows.

1.   Connect the red (R) pin to the Material node's Ambient Occlusion pin.

2.   Connect the green (G) pin to the Material node's Roughness pin.

3.   Connect the blue (B) pin to the Material node's Metallic pin.

Your setup should look similar to Figure 9-16.

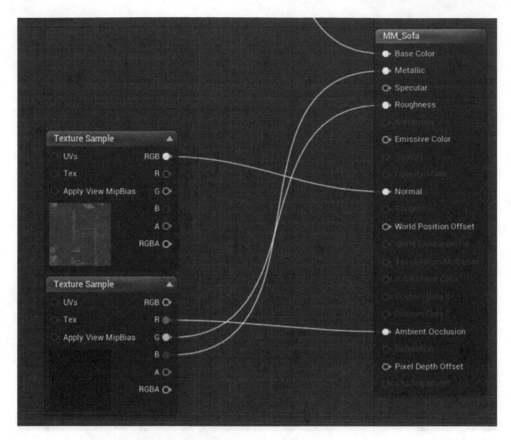

Figure 9-16. *Setup for ORM texture*

You can multiply the ORM texture's green channel by a parameter to control the roughness of your asset. Simply create a parameter named Roughness and add a Multiply node. Connect them as shown in Figure 9-17. Do this by dragging away the B node on the new Multiply node and searching for param. Then select the Scalar parameter and rename it Roughness.

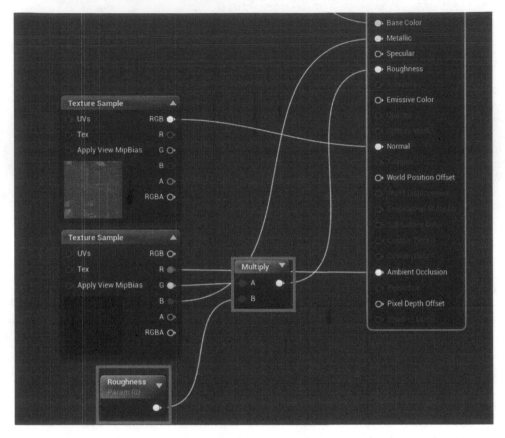

Figure 9-17. *Setup for controlling Roughness*

Applying the Material to a Mesh

Once you have saved your material, you are ready to apply it to your mesh. Drag and drop the material from the Content Browser to the asset on your scene. It should be textured, as you did in Substance Painter. The result depends on what you created, but Figure 9-18 shows the result from my scene.

Figure 9-18. *Result of applying material*

When working on architectural design visualization, you may have to use an asset that plays a role with other assets to create a complete scene. Figures 9-19 through 9-22 are previews of a render using three copies of a sofa placed in a design visualization interior set.

Figure 9-19. *Long shot 1 scene*

Figure 9-20. *Long shot 2 scene*

Figure 9-21. *Long shot 3 scene*

Figure 9-22. *Long shot 4 scene*

This chapter concludes with these results.

In the next chapter, you create more materials and work with master and instanced materials.

CHAPTER 10

Real-Time Emissive Materials

You have created standard materials. Now let's look at creating real-time emissive materials. In this chapter, you also create instanced materials and learn their importance.

Master and Instanced Materials

Let's look at the sofa material that you created in the last chapter. You named it MM_ Sofa. The MM stands for *master material*. Master material is the main or parent material that contains all the maps and calculations required to build material. Instanced material creates minor variations to the master material by using parameters that you expose in the related master material. An instanced material is the child of a master material. An instanced material allows you to make quick adjustments to the master material without having to recompile the entire material. You can create multiple child instances of the same master material, each one having a different look.

Let's demonstrate the need for instanced materials. Suppose you wish to change the color of the sofa. Open your sofa master material, and using the Tint node, select a color (see Figure 10-1).

© Abhishek Kumar 2021
A. Kumar, *Immersive 3D Design Visualization*, https://doi.org/10.1007/978-1-4842-6597-0_10

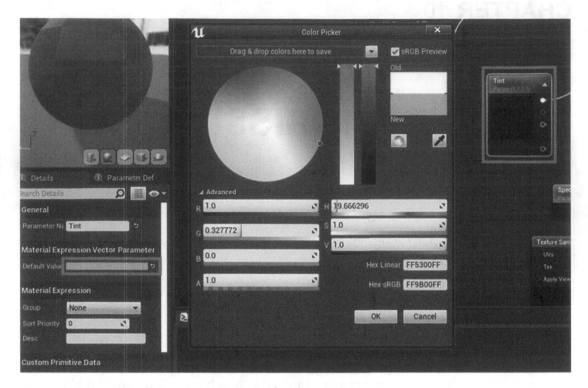

Figure 10-1. *Changing the color of our material*

Click the Save button (see Figure 10-2).

Figure 10-2. *Saving changes to asset*

The save takes time, depending on the material's complexity. Making a change like this in the master material if certainly *not recommended* because it takes a long time to compile. You can share multiple instanced materials from a single master. Any changes may negatively alter every instanced material. It is not convenient, but there is a better way to make minor changes. It is by creating an instanced material.

Right-click MM_Sofa in the Content Browser and select Create Material Instance from the list (see Figure 10-3). Name this material M_Sofa.

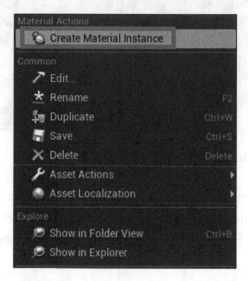

Figure 10-3. *Creating a material instance*

Once the material instance has been created, drag and drop it from the Content Browser and onto your sofa mesh. After that, double-click it to reveal its settings. The parameter nodes that you created in the last chapter are here as editable settings (see Figure 10-4).

Figure 10-4. *Material instance window*

If you want to make any changes to the parameters, you must enable them by clicking the check boxes next to each of their names and then setting the desired values. Let's do that now. Enable Tint and Roughness and set their values, as shown in Figure 10-5.

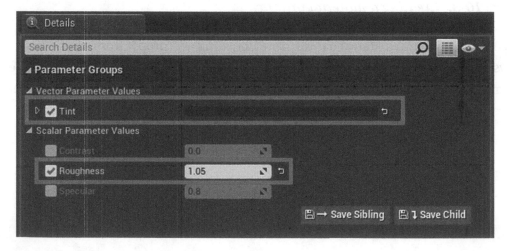

Figure 10-5. *Editing instanced material*

You immediately see the changes that you made without any load or compile time. Figure 10-6 shows the changed look of the sofa resulting from the adjustments that you made.

Figure 10-6. *Resulting outcome*

If you want multiple sofas of different colors in your scene, simply make multiple instances of your sofa master material. Make sure to make instances of your master material only. This is very important; otherwise, you may have an unwanted outcome. If you create an instance of another instanced material, then any changes you make to the previous one affects its child. The master material is kept constant so that you can make as many variations from it as you want. Drag and drop the different variations of instanced materials to the assets in your scene.

Creating Emissive Materials

Let's create an emissive material. It is a type of material that glows or emits light on its own. It gives a nice look to an environment. In our case, they will make the light meshes appear to be on. Creating an emissive material is simple in UE4. All you need is an image that tells the UE4 which parts of your mesh need to have the emissive effect. This is called an *emissive map*; it is usually a grayscale image. The white parts represent the glowing areas, and the black parts represent the non-emissive areas on the mesh (see Figure 10-7).

Figure 10-7. *A very simple emissive map*

Creating one is very easy. All you need is an image-editing software like Photoshop or GIMP, or even the default Paint application that comes with Windows. As you may have already guessed, you just need to paint some areas of your UV map white, and the rest of the areas remain black. For this example, let's use a simple UV unwrapped lamp shape (see Figure 10-8). Let's use Maya to create our mesh and UVs.

Figure 10-8. *Simple lamp shape*

You want the bottom-facing face to produce light, as you see in flat lamps like these. Select the UV shell and move it as shown in Figure 10-9.

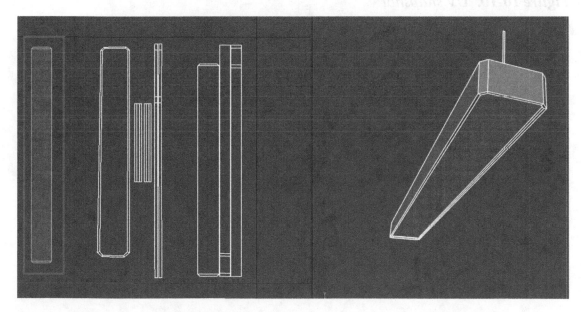

Figure 10-9. *Place the glowing face*

Let's export this UV by clicking Image ➤ UV Snapshot (see Figure 10-10).

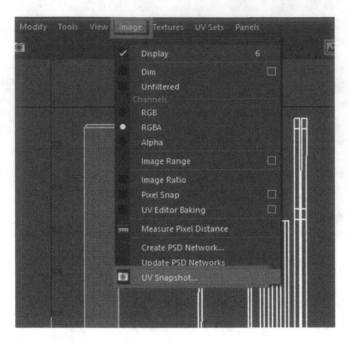

Figure 10-10. *UV snapshot*

In the UV Snapshot Options panel, set Image Format to PNG and Size to 1024, and then save (somewhere convenient) (see Figure 10-11).

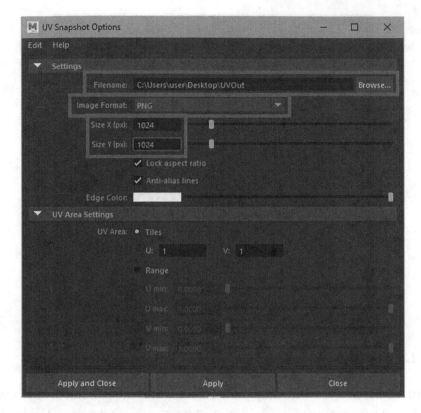

Figure 10-11. *Image snapshot settings*

Open it in the image-editing application of your choice. Since this takes barely a minute to do, you can use Windows Paint to paint the image, as shown in Figure 10-12.

Figure 10-12. *Hand-painted emissive map*

Figure 10-12 shows the entire map painted black and the general area where the UV shell of the face that needs to glow is painted white. You need this map later in UE4, so save it as a TGA file in a convenient location. Export the lamp model from Maya as SM_Lamp_S (SM stands for *static mesh*) in FBX format. Next, apply a generic metal material on this mesh using Substance Painter (refer to Chapter 8). Then, return to UE4. Import your mesh into a Lamp_S folder. Right-click and duplicate the sofa master material and move it to the Lamp_S folder.

Rename the duplicated sofa master material MM_Lamps. Double-click to open it. Replace the sofa materials with the lamp materials. Drag and drop the emissive map that you created into the Content Browser and then into the material editor. Plug it into the Emissive Color channel, as shown in Figure 10-13.

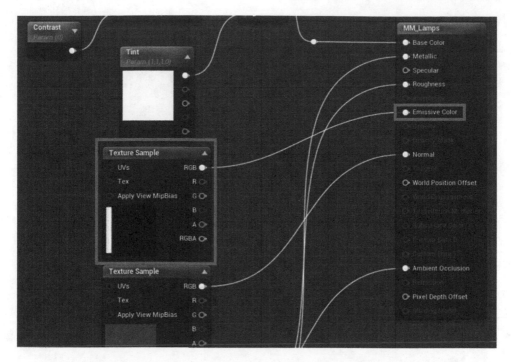

Figure 10-13. *Plugging emissive map into Emissive Color input*

Save and apply this material on your mesh and see what happens. Your result should look somewhat similar to Figure 10-14.

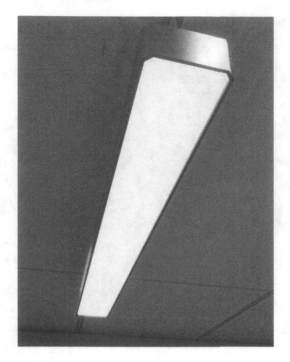

Figure 10-14. *Results so far*

As you can see in Figure 10-14, our lamp is barely glowing. Let's fix that. Add a Multiply node and a Constant node. Convert the constant into a parameter and name it Emissive_Intensity. Connect them as shown in Figure 10-15.

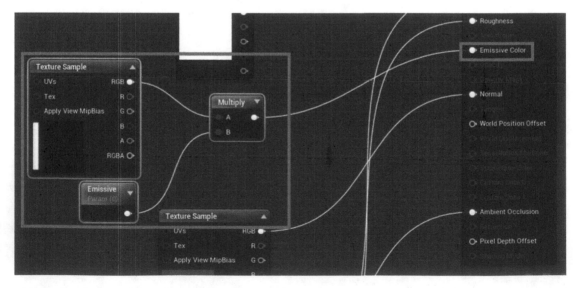

Figure 10-15. *Connection setup*

Save and create a material from this and name it M_Lamps. Next, drag and drop it on the mesh. Double-click to open the M_Lamps settings and enable the Emissive_Intensity parameter. Set its value to a high number like 10 (see Figure 10-16).

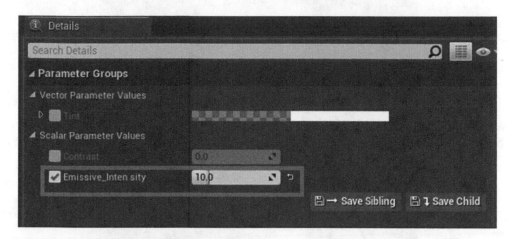

Figure 10-16. *Increasing Emissive Intensity*

Now your lamp should produce a bright glow, similar to what's shown in Figure 10-17.

Figure 10-17. *Emissive glow from our mesh*

The next chapter explores the object properties editor in depth.

CHAPTER 11

Importing Assets in Detail

You have already imported assets into UE4, but you haven't explored all the tools in depth. This chapter is dedicated to the important settings and functions available as you import your assets and modify asset properties after they have been imported.

Import Settings for Assets

When importing assets, the Import Options panel provides several important settings. Drag and drop the Headset asset into the UE4 Content Browser. Now, let's look at the Import settings. Figure 11-1 highlights some important settings that are discussed in this chapter.

© Abhishek Kumar 2021
A. Kumar, *Immersive 3D Design Visualization*, https://doi.org/10.1007/978-1-4842-6597-0_11

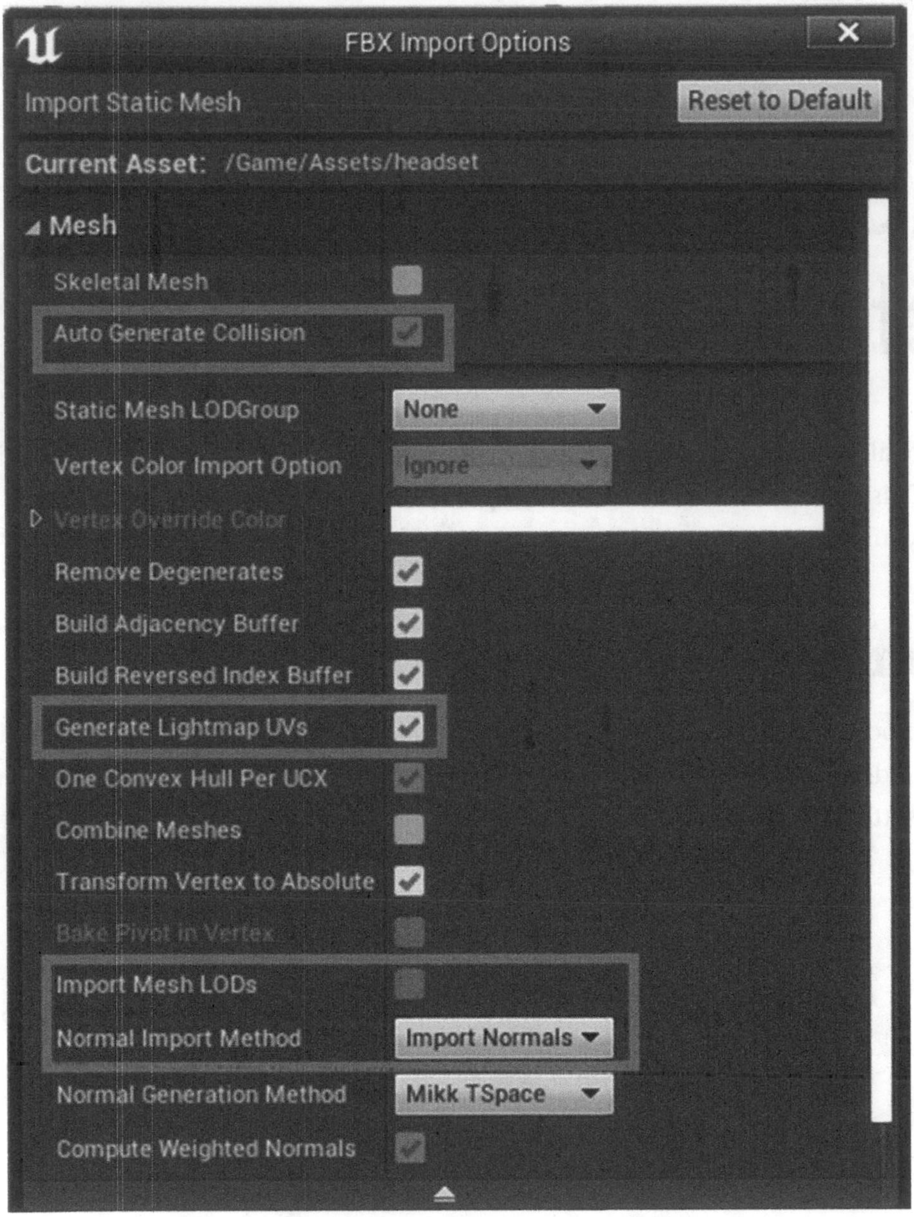

Figure 11-1. *Some important import settings*

Let's discuss them one by one. Auto Generate Collisions is a setting that you have already indirectly seen in action when assembling our first level. Automatic collisions generate rough collision data for meshes imported into UE4, if you haven't created a collision on your own or if you are testing out assets. It does quick and rough work, and typically, it does not produce good collisions for complex meshes. You can see the collision of meshes by double-clicking them in the Content Browser. In the Asset Details window, click Collision and enable Simple Collision (see Figure 11-2).

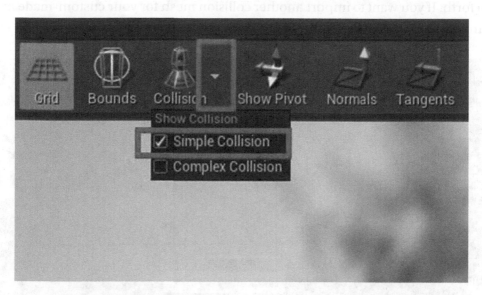

Figure 11-2. *Enabling collision display*

You should see the outline of the collision on your mesh, as shown in Figure 11-3.

Figure 11-3. *Outline of the collision*

As you can see, the collision has problems. An autogenerated simple collision covers the mesh's general bounds instead of accurately tracing the shape of the object. It is good only when testing assets or for very simple assets like walls or floors that have no "holes" and so forth. If you want to import another collision mesh for your custom-made mesh, you can import it by clicking Complex Collision Mesh under Collision (see Figure 11-4).

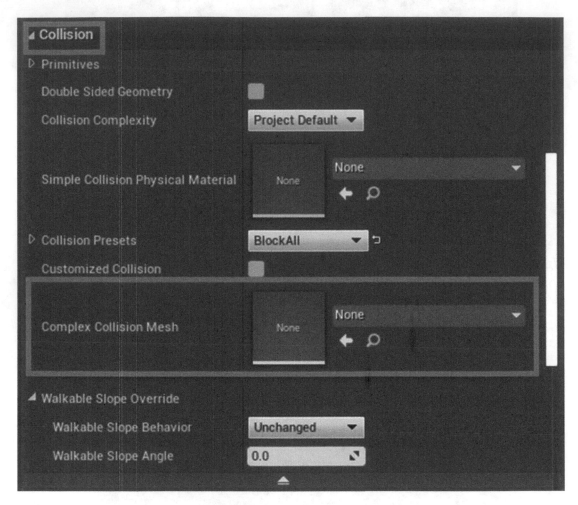

Figure 11-4. *Assigning custom collision mesh*

Generating Automatic Lightmap UVs and Other Settings

Let's look at Generate Lightmap UVs. Lightmaps for assets are always generated in the DCC application. This option is disabled when you are importing assets because it is redundant most of the time. But when you are working on a white-box or test level, it is useful because you are not very concerned about the quality. It provides automatic creation of lightmaps when you want to quickly prototype a map or develop a simple level design. You can check your lightmap UV by clicking UV and (typically) selecting UV Channel 1 (see Figure 11-5).

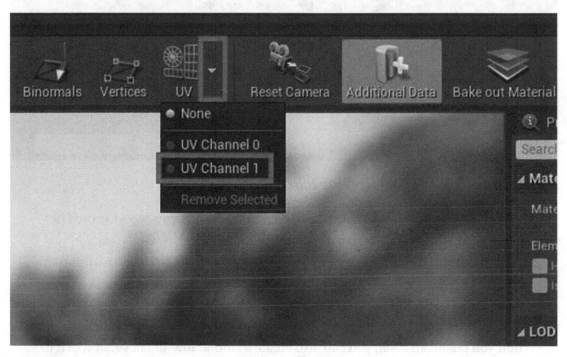

***Figure 11-5.** Checking our UV channel*

To determine your Lightmap UV channel, check Destination Lightmap Index under Build Settings (see Figure 11-6).

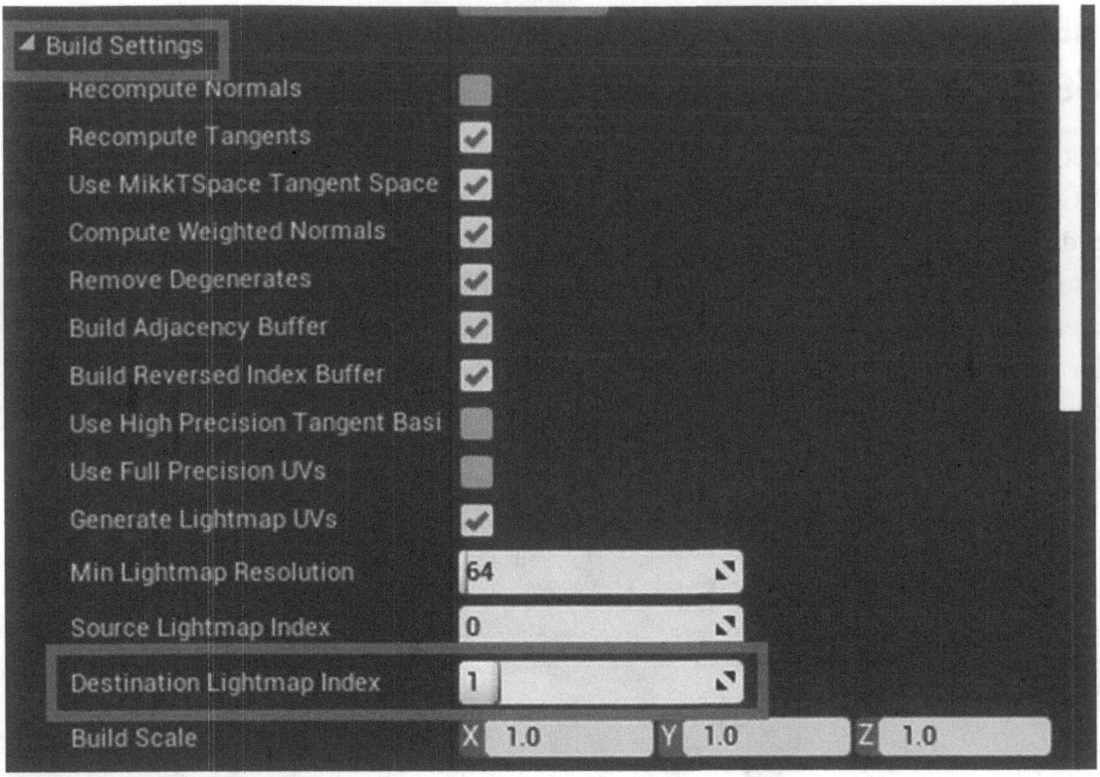

Figure 11-6. *Destination Lightmap Index*

The lightmap index starts at 0 and goes up. The index that you see +1 is the UV channel number that your lightmap is located in.

Next, let's look at Import Mesh LODs. An LOD, or Level of Detail, is an important aspect of game assets. A game asset can render in full detail when a player is close to the asset. But when a player moves far away from that asset, and it is barely visible, there is no reason for it to have the same amount of detail as it does when it is close to the player.

When you create an asset, you can also create a similar low-detail version of it to use as the LOD. An asset can have multiple LOD models, each one with a diminishing amount of polycount and detail. When imported into UE4, you can set up the fade distance of the asset. This determines the distance when an asset starts to fade into its low-detail version as the player moves further away from it.

You can import LOD assets by going to LOD Settings and clicking LOD Import (see Figure 11-7).

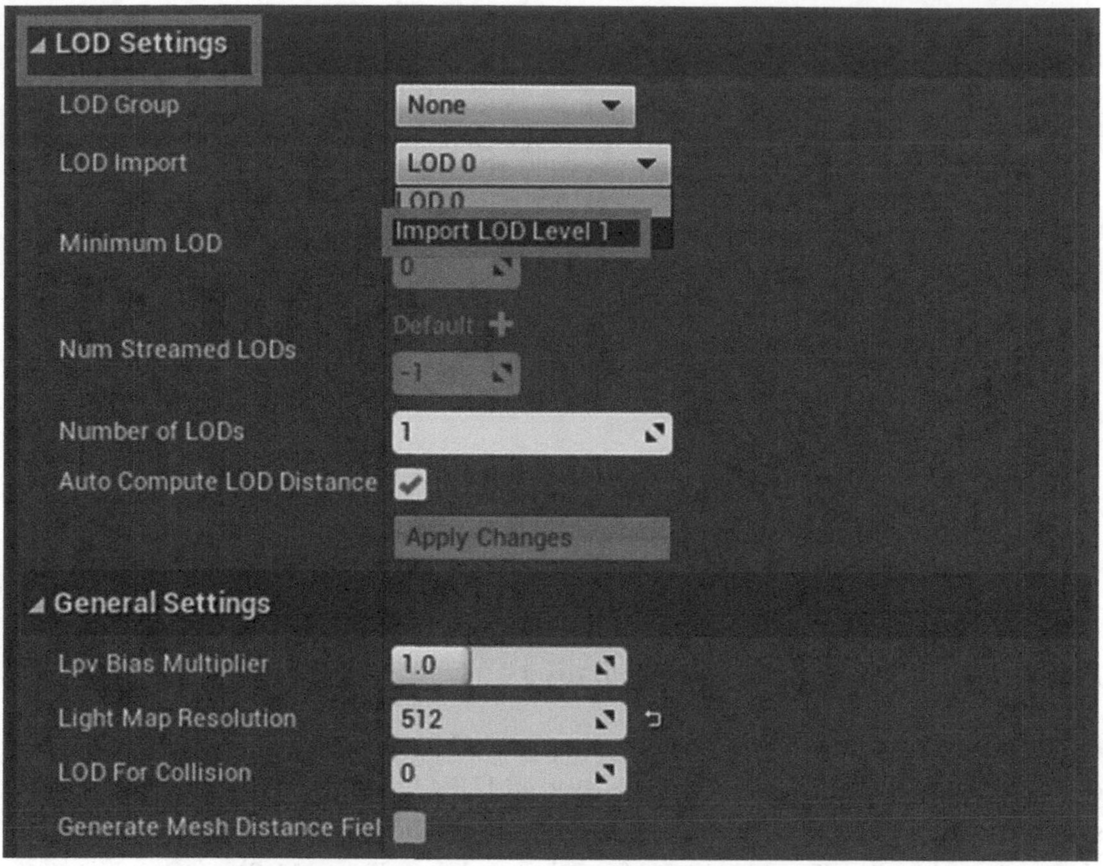

Figure 11-7. Import LOD

Once the LOD has been imported, it has a default loading distance set. Save
your asset and zoom away to see the LOD mesh that you chose to load. If you don't
have an LOD model, then UE4 has a built-in LOD generation tool that you can use to
automatically decimate the details in your model. First, check the number of polygons
on the mesh in the top-right corner of the screen (see Figure 11-8).

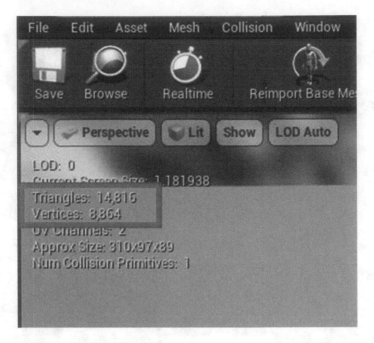

Figure 11-8. *Current polycount of our asset*

Under LOD Settings, go to the LOD group and select Deco from the list. This means our asset is categorized as a Decoration asset, and UE4 has an LOD preset set for it. Now save the asset, and try flying away from it. You see that the LOD number and polycount change based on the distance you are from the mesh (see Figure 11-9).

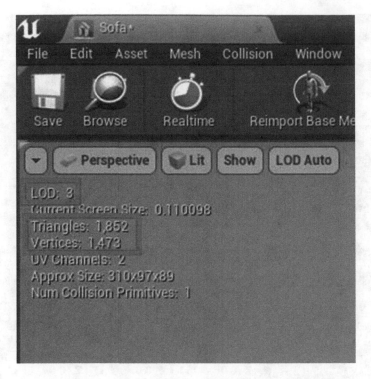

Figure 11-9. *LOD number and polycount changes*

Let's now look at the Normal Import Method. If you click its drop-down menu, you see three suboptions (see Figure 11-10).

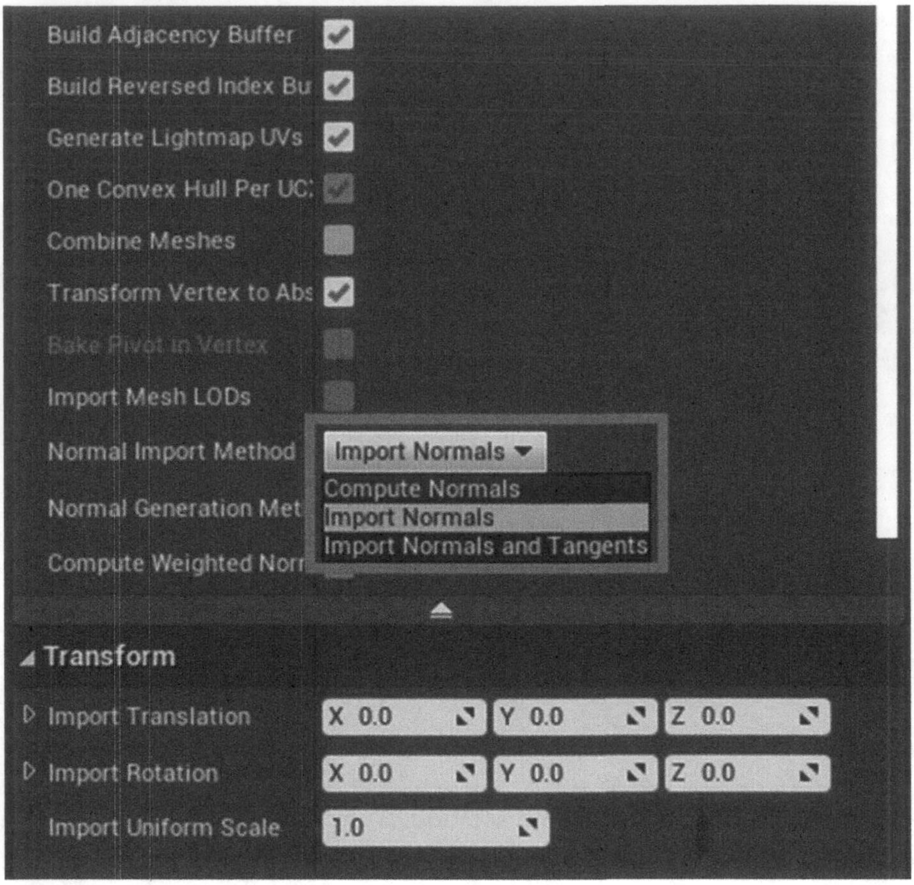

Figure 11-10. *Normal Import Methods*

Each option has a different effect. The default is Import Normals, which imports the normal data stored in the mesh and generates only tangent information in UE4. The normal and smoothing group is something that you create in the DCC application. The Import Normals option simply imports everything that your mesh has already stored.

Compute Normals overrides the normal information stored on the mesh and generates new information in UE4. This includes smoothing groups and tangent information.

The Import Normals and Tangents option imports all the smoothing group and tangent data stored directly in the imported mesh, and nothing is calculated internally.

Each of these options has use cases. Generally, it is best to remain in the default Import Normals method.

That's all for this chapter. In the next chapter, you utilize all the information you have learned so far to create a small scene using all the assets.

CHAPTER 12

Creating a Level

Previously, you created a basic level and learned how to use basic shapes to block out an idea. In this chapter, you create a very basic level, but with more details this time. Let's begin by creating a rectangular area, which will be our room, and then populate it with some simple assets. After that, let's bring in the headset that you created in previous chapters, and then finally, light our scene.

Importing a Quixel Megascans Texture

You saw in a previous chapter how to download and install Quixel Bridge and set it up for UE4. Let's now look at how to send textures from Bridge to UE4 and use them in our scenes. First, make sure that both UE4 and Bridge are running. Then, in UE4, run the Quixel plugin by clicking the Megascans icon (see Figure 12-1).

Figure 12-1. *Megascans plugin*

© Abhishek Kumar 2021

A. Kumar, *Immersive 3D Design Visualization*, https://doi.org/10.1007/978-1-4842-6597-0_12

Once the Megascans window launchs, switch to the Quixel Bridge application. Select a texture to export to UE4 and click Download. Let's say you chose a modern tile floor texture (see Figure 12-2).

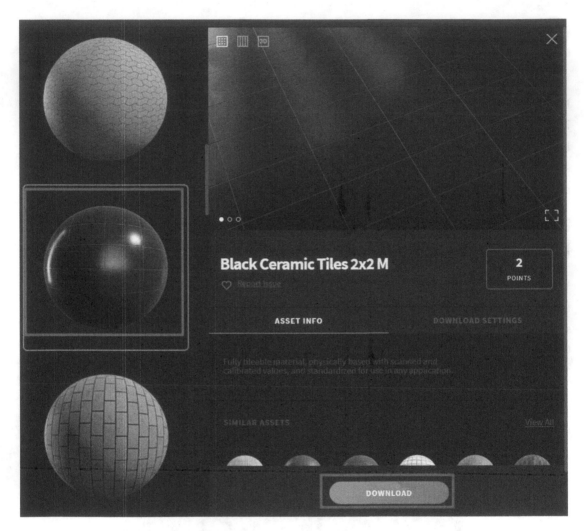

Figure 12-2. *Choosing material*

Once the asset has downloaded, you see all the export options (see Figure 12-3).

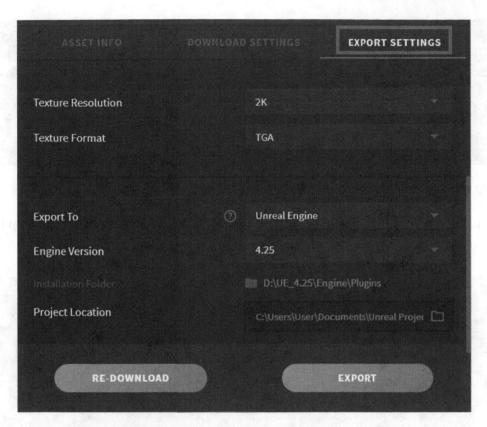

Figure 12-3. *Export settings*

Figure 12-3 shows Texture Resolution set to 2K and Texture Format set to TGA. These are the best settings for UE4. Once you have chosen the directory location to save your project, click EXPORT to send the material to UE4. After a brief export process, you find the material in the Megascans/Surfaces folder in the Content Browser (see Figure 12-4).

Figure 12-4. *Material exported to UE4*

The material is set up automatically for you. All you have to do is drag and drop it onto the mesh that you want to apply it (see Figure 12-5).

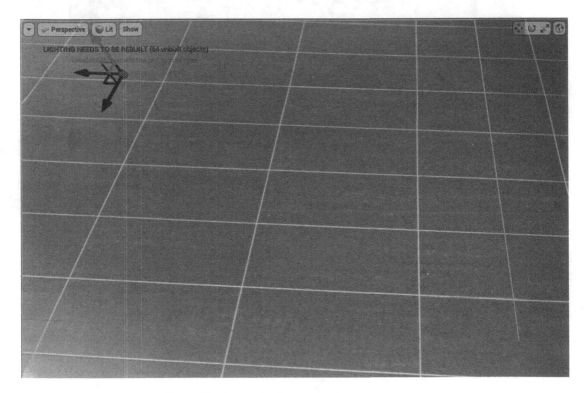

Figure 12-5. *Material applied to our floor mesh*

The following are materials to use for this project.

- Terrazzo Floor 2×2 M

- Wall Plaster 2×2 M

- Smooth Concrete Blocks 2×2 M

- Cat Palm if you want a 3D plant to decorate your scene

Now create a simple room with ten walls and six floors, as shown in Figure 12-6.

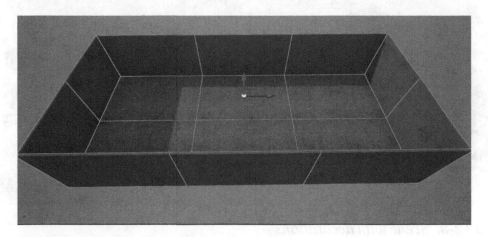

Figure 12-6. *Room setup*

Let's apply Megascans materials on our meshes, as shown in Figure 12-7.

Figure 12-7. *Materials applied to our mesh*

Next, drag in the sofas, tables, and decorations and place them in the scene (see Figure 12-8).

Figure 12-8. *Scene with decorations*

Next, let's export the headset model from Substance Painter. Export using the UE4 preset and targa image format (see Figure 12-9).

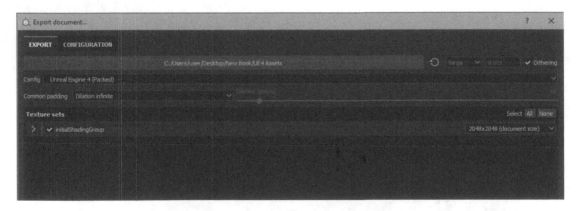

Figure 12-9. *Export settings*

Once done, create a folder for the headset asset in the UE4 Content Browser, and drag and drop the exported mesh and materials into this folder. Set up your material the same way you did in the previous chapter (see Figure 12-10).

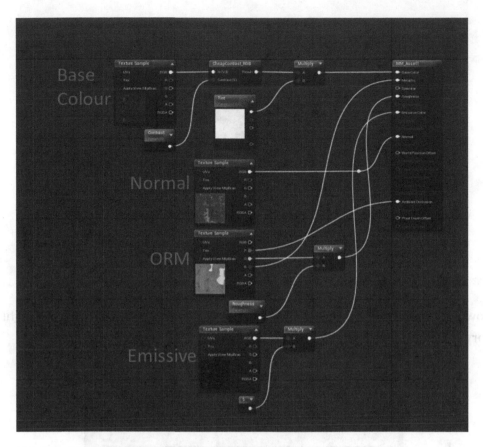

Figure 12-10. *Material setup for the headset*

Drag and drop the headset into the scene. Place it on the sofa and then apply the material to it. The result should look something like Figure 12-11.

Figure 12-11. *Headset asset*

Now add some basic lighting to the scene. In the Place Actors panel, in the Lights category, find Spot Light (see Figure 12-12).

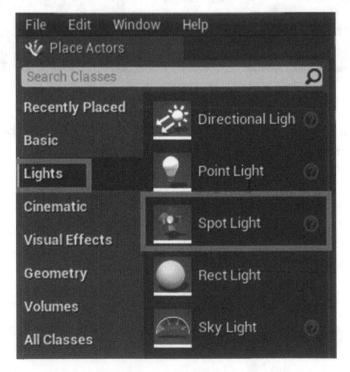

Figure 12-12. *Spot Light actor*

Next, set the light settings, as shown in Figure 12-13.

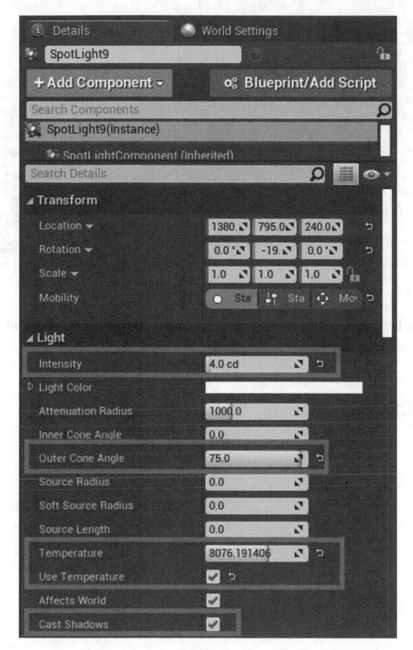

Figure 12-13. *Light settings*

Position the light slightly slanting toward the wall, as shown in Figure 12-14.

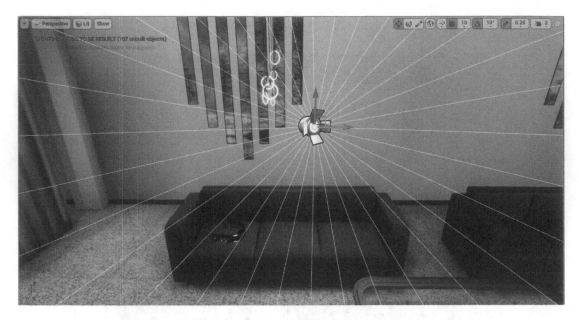

Figure 12-14. *Positioning the light*

Copy the light around the scene if you want better illumination. Once you are done, do a light bake.

Final Renders

Figures 12-15 through 12-17 show the results.

Figure 12-15. *Final result 1*

Figure 12-16. *Final result 2*

Figure 12-17. *Final result 3*

That's it for this chapter.

In the next chapter, you locate and fix some common errors.

CHAPTER 13

Testing and Fixing Errors

In the previous chapter, you created a very basic level. Now let's fix some common errors that occur. Most of them are related to lighting. There are various ways to tackle every problem, so in this chapter, I share the methods that I use when certain problems arise.

Lighting Problems

When you work with modular assets, it is common to encounter lighting problems like the one shown in Figure 13-1.

Figure 13-1. *Light leaking*

© Abhishek Kumar 2021
A. Kumar, *Immersive 3D Design Visualization*, https://doi.org/10.1007/978-1-4842-6597-0_13

You can see a small beam of light leaking through the wall, which looks wrong. Something like this usually happens when there is a gap or hole somewhere in the mesh, and everything is not watertight. If you look around the mesh, you may see something like what's shown in Figure 13-2.

Figure 13-2. *Gaps between meshes*

But if you look at it from the other side, there is no gap, as seen in Figure 13-3.

Figure 13-3. *No visible gaps in the mesh*

This is due to *backface culling*, which means that only one side of a mesh face is rendered, and the other side is *culled*, meaning it was not rendered. You can simply see through it, and thus any light in the scene passes through the culled side of the face.

The way to fix it in this case is to simply close the gap by overlapping the meshes, as shown in Figure 13-4.

Figure 13-4. *Overlapping our mesh*

This results in *z-fighting* in the overlapping areas, which means the overlapping faces flicker because UE4 is confused about which one to render on top of the other one. But this is fine in our case because this happens where the players cannot see. If this happens in a visible area, however, you should fix it by carefully moving the meshes so that overlapping does not happen.

Shadow Seam Problems

Let's look at shadow seam issues and how to fix them. In the previous chapter, you changed lightmass settings to reduce the shadow seam effect. Figure 13-5 shows the settings once again.

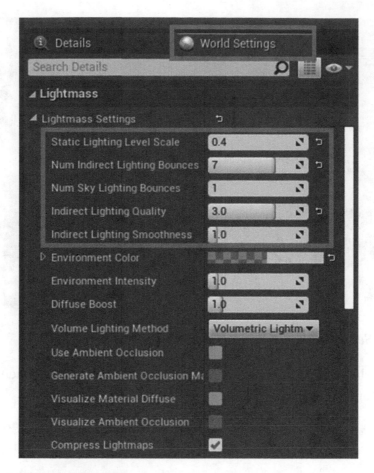

Figure 13-5. Lightmass settings

Building light with these settings means a lower number of light seams appear. But if this doesn't correctly solve the problem, there is one more tool at our disposal. Select the walls with shadow seams, as shown in Figure 13-6.

Figure 13-6. *Selecting the walls with seam issues*

Next, right-click any of the selected walls to open the Asset actions menu. In this menu, select Merge Actors, as shown in Figure 13-7.

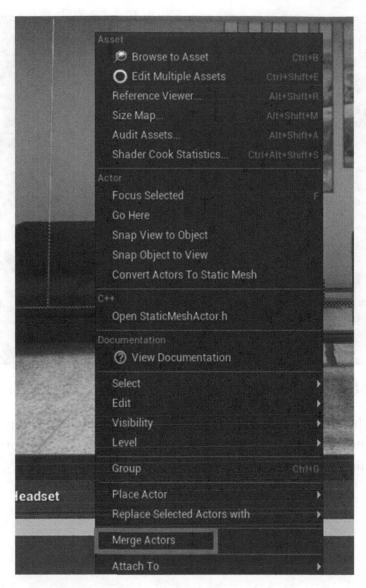

Figure 13-7. *Merge actors*

In the Merge Actors settings panel, go to Mesh Replacement Method, select Remove Original Actors, and click the Merge Actors button (see Figure 13-8).

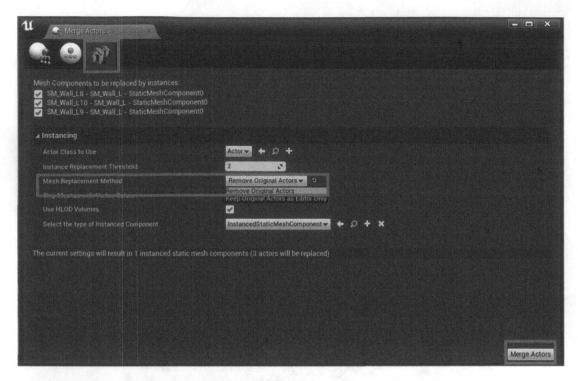

Figure 13-8. *Merge actor settings*

Once done, bake your lights again. The shadow seams should no longer appear. Merging actors not only removes problems like this but also optimizes your scene. Figure 13-9 is a final look at the wall.

Figure 13-9. *Shadow seams removed*

That's it for this chapter. Hopefully, you are now able to solve these common problems in your scene.

In the next chapter, you extend and complete the scene.

CHAPTER 14

Design Visualization Capstone Project: Aesthetic Development

You have created a simple level, set up basic lighting, and fixed some common errors that occur in projects like these. In this chapter, you extend the level and apply the final lighting setup. Let's get started.

Extending the Level

So far, our level is very basic. You are going to extend it some more. First, let's look at our map's rough layout from a top-down view (see Figure 14-1).

A. Kumar, *Immersive 3D Design Visualization*, https://doi.org/10.1007/978-1-4842-6597-0_14

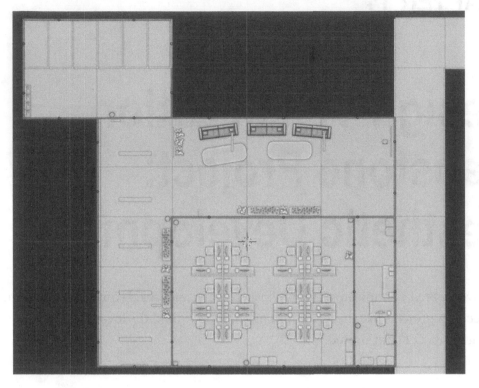

Figure 14-1. *The layout of our room*

As you can see, it is an office-like environment, and some extra assets have been used. Once again, you are using the UE4 snapping system. Set the snapping to 10 units and extend your previously created room to create a hallway, as shown in Figure 14-2.

Figure 14-2. *Placing walls*

Let's add some windows to the extended hallway, as shown in Figure 14-3.

Figure 14-3. *Adding windows to our hallway*

Next, add the walls for the other areas, as shown in Figure 14-1. Then, add the decoration items. The interior areas of our scene are dark because they don't have any lighting. To work on these scenes, switch to Unlit mode by clicking the Unlit option shown in Figure 14-4.

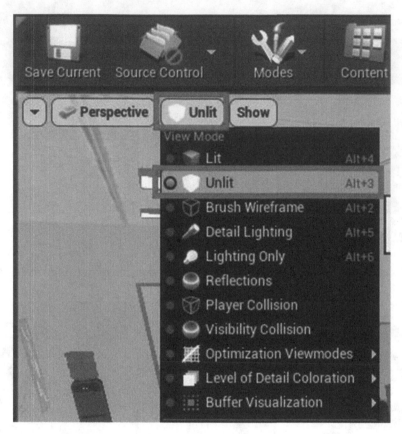

Figure 14-4. *Switching to Unlit mode*

In Unlit mode, start adding some lights to your scene. Duplicate the light you previously created by holding the Alt key and dragging it along any axis. Once you duplicate the light, place it under every light model, as shown in Figure 14-5.

Figure 14-5. *Placing light actors*

After this, bake the lights to see the result. If there is darkness in places, add more lights to make it as bright as you want. My results are shown in Figures 14-6 and Figure 14-7.

Figure 14-6. *Reception area view*

If your PC is struggling to handle so many lights, there are alternative solutions. Try increasing the intensity of the lights and increasing the Attenuation Radius value even more. You can also disable Use Inverse Square Falloff so that light retains its strength over a longer range. This requires some trial and error and playing with values. It is something that you can try as a last resort if you face serious performance issues.

Figure 14-7. *Office work area*

Adding Final Touches

Let's now work on some final touches in our level. When you want a reflective surface in your scene, you need to add a *reflection capture*. Go to Place Actors, and use the search tab to search for *reflection* (see Figure 14-8).

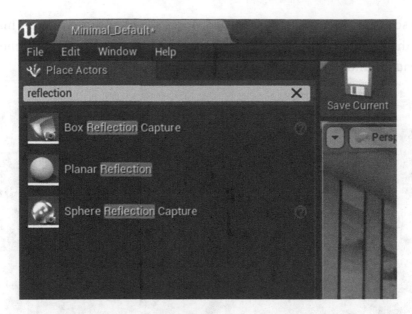

Figure 14-8. *Search for Reflection Capture*

Drag and drop Sphere Reflection Capture into your scene. You can see the bounds of this actor in the scene (see Figure 14-9).

Figure 14-9. *Bounds of reflection capture*

271

You can scale up the actor to increase the size of the bounding sphere. This determines the number of meshes in your scene that it affects. A normal scene requires several spread around the scene, as shown in Figure 14-10.

Figure 14-10. *Sphere Reflection Captures in the scene*

You can create mirrors using planar reflection in the same way. Drag and drop Planar Reflection into your scene and scale it so that it covers the general surface of a mirror (see Figure 14-11).

Figure 14-11. *Adding planar reflection*

Add a glass see-through view, as shown in Figure 14-12.

Figure 14-12. *Glass see-through view*

Finally, a gallery view is seen in Figure 14-13.

Figure 14-13. *Gallery view*

That's it for this design visualization chapter.

In the next chapter, you close this book with some final tips and suggestions, and a portfolio presentation.

CHAPTER 15

Immersive Design Portfolio

You have a level and lighting set up. In this chapter, you clean up and finalize everything. At the end, I give you some final advice on how to proceed with your journey in this field.

Cleaning up and Previewing Our Scene

Go through your Content Browser and find any assets that you have imported but did not use. It's common to import Marketplace packages that contain lots of extra assets that you don't end up using. You can go through and delete these from your project to reduce its size. If you have any Starter Content files that you don't need, simply delete them (see Figure 15-1).

© Abhishek Kumar 2021
A. Kumar, *Immersive 3D Design Visualization*, https://doi.org/10.1007/978-1-4842-6597-0_15

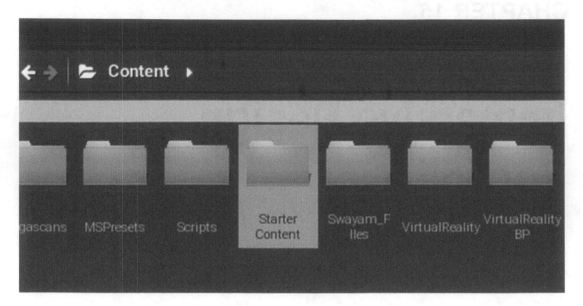

Figure 15-1. *Deleting unwanted files*

Let's now preview our scene from the first-person perspective. You can click Play (see Figure 15-2) or press Alt+P to start playing your scene.

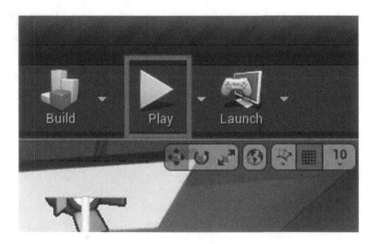

Figure 15-2. *Play a scene*

You can move around the scene like a player would experience it. To play the scene in VR, you need to have a VR headset connected to your PC. Click the arrow next to Play, and you should see the VR Preview option, as shown in Figure 15-3.

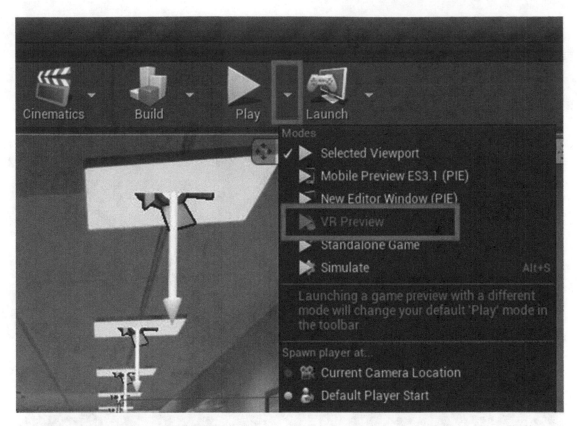

Figure 15-3. *VR Preview option*

Interactive Simulation

There are several doors in the scene, as you can see in the images. In this section, you create the interaction system for opening and closing them. This is a very simple setup requiring two key components. First, two meshes named Door Frame and Door. itself (You can find these in UE4's Starter Content if you don't have your own meshes). Second, a simple physics setup with constraints to control the movement.

Let's begin by adding a door frame in a suitable place, as shown in Figure 15-4.

Figure 15-4. *Adding a door frame*

Next, add a door mesh to the door frame, as shown in Figure 15-5.

Figure 15-5. *Adding a door mesh*

Next, double-click the door mesh in the Content Browser to open the Asset details window. Here, click Collision and enable Simple Collision to visualize the bounds of the collision. Select and delete whatever default collision you have (see Figure 15-6). It should appear as a green box.

Figure 15-6. *Visualize and delete the default collision.*

Next, add Simplified Box Collision by clicking Collision ➤ Add Box Simplified Collision (see Figure 15-7).

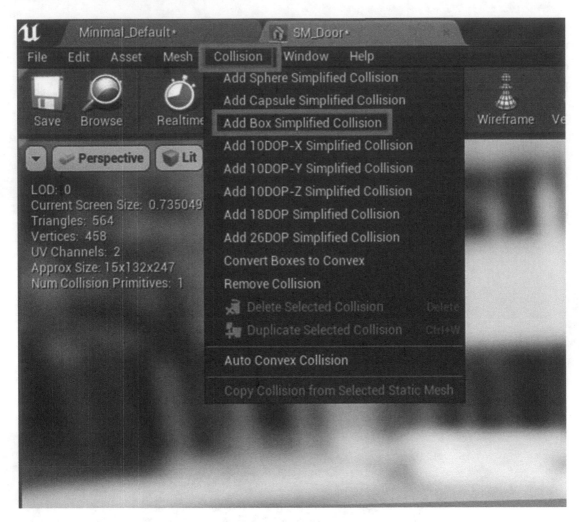

Figure 15-7. *Add a simple box collision to the mesh.*

Select the simple box collision, press R, and scale it down, as shown in Figure 15-8. Scale it down small enough so that the collisions for the wall and the door frame around it don't interfere with it.

Figure 15-8. *Scaling the collision*

In the Details panel on the right-hand side, scroll down until you see the Collision tab. Under it, make sure that Collision Complexity is set to Project Default. Next, set Collision Preset to Custom (see Figure 15-9).

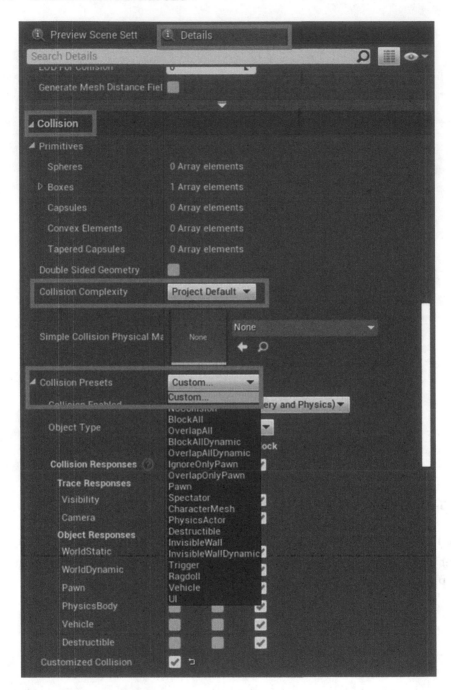

Figure 15-9. *Collision settings*

Under Collision Responses, set PhysicsBody to Ignore by clicking the check box, as shown in Figure 15-10.

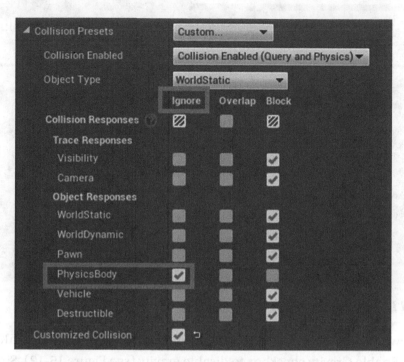

Figure 15-10. *Settings collision response of PhysicsBody*

You're all done here, so click Save in the top-left corner to save all the settings.

Select the door that you added to the scene. In the Details panel, set Mobility to Movable, which allows the door to cast dynamic shadows and prevent light from baking into it from a fixed location (see Figure 15-11). This has nothing to do with physics; it is purely for lighting purposes. You can completely ignore this step if you don't want dynamic shadows and prefer performance over visuals. Alternatively, you can set this to Stationary for a middle ground between static and dynamic.

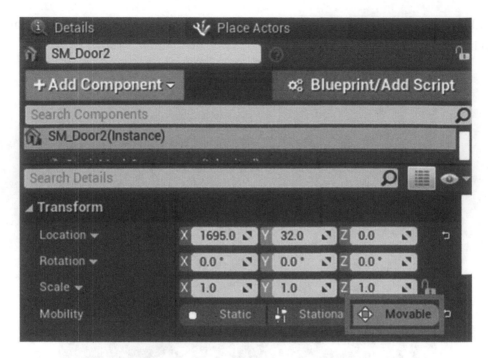

Figure 15-11. *Setting the mesh to Movable*

Scroll down. Under the Physics tab, enable Simulate Physics and MassInKg, and uncheck the Enable Gravity checkbox to disable gravity (see Figure 15-12). Simulate Physics makes our bodies simulate physics, as the name suggests. MassInKg allows you to set body weight. And you disable gravity because you don't want our mesh to be affected by gravity because it produces undesirable effects.

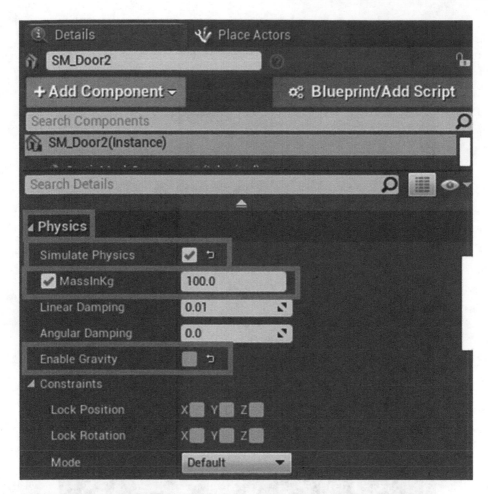

Figure 15-12. *Physics settings-1*

Let's increase MassInKg to a high number like 300 because you want the door to feel
heavy. However, it may seem like an absurd weight for a door by real-world standards,
but in UE4, this is what feels normal. Next, increase Angular Damping to a number
like 6 or 7. This adds resistance to the rotation of the door, as if there is friction and air
resistance, and other factors from the real world (see Figure 15-13).

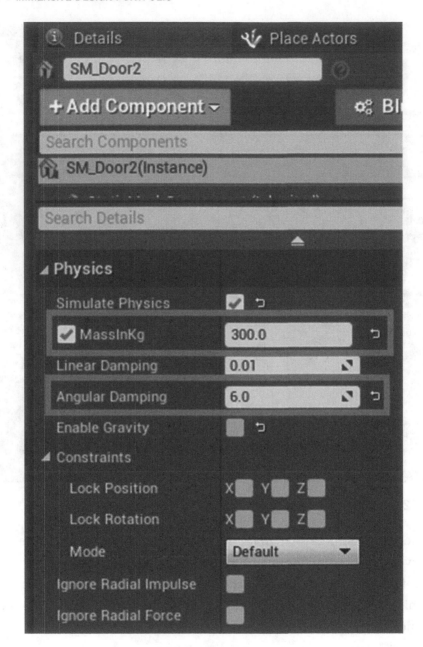

Figure 15-13. *Set MassInKg and Angular Damping*

When our player collides with the door, you want the door to rotate, but with the current settings, the door simply flies backward when you touch it. Play your level to test this now. You need to constraint this object to rotate along only the Z axis when you touch it. Why the Z axis? Select and rotate your door by pressing the E key on all three axes. Notice that rotation along the Z axis feels like the most normal rotation of the door.

Now, let's activate the relevant constraints on our door. First, lock its position on all X, Y, and Z axes on which the door is hinged so that they can't move from their positions. Under the Physics tab, find Constraints. Click all the X, Y, and Z check boxes next to Lock Position. Also, you want the rotation to happen only along the Z axis, so click the X and Y check boxes next to Lock Rotation. Your settings should look similar to Figure 15-14.

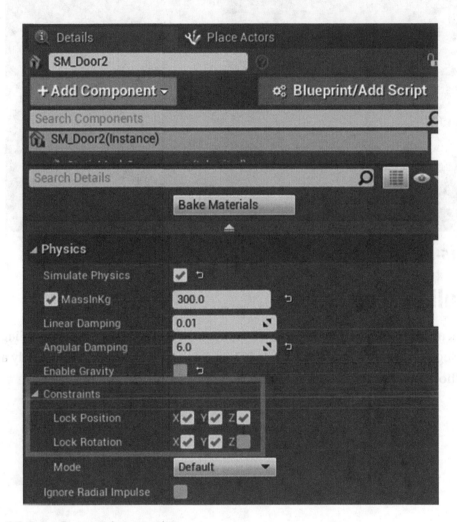

Figure 15-14. *Constraints settings*

Now play your level and try pushing your door. You see that your door can now be pushed and open naturally like a real door, as shown in Figure 15-15.

Figure 15-15. *Physics enabled door*

Portfolio Presentation

Let's look at some shots of the render and analyze them. Figure 15-16 shows foliage from Quixel Megascans. They are ready-made 3D assets that can be imported directly and used without much hassle.

Figure 15-16. *Foliage assets from Quixel Megascans*

Next, let's look at the glass material in the scene. It is called Advanced Glass Material Pack, which is part of a free asset pack available in the UE4 marketplace (see Figure 15-17).

Figure 15-17. *Glass material*

The same glass material is shown in Figure 15-18.

Figure 15-18. *Glass material for a large window*

Figures 15-19 and 15-20 show a long shot of a bathroom. The attempt is to capture everything that has been put in there.

Figure 15-19. *Bathroom long shot*

Figure 15-20. *Top angle of the bathroom*

Next is the office room with all the computers and furniture. There are a lot of duplicated objects here, as you can see. This is the advantage of a modular design. You can populate an entire scene with fewer assets (see Figures 15-21 and 15-22).

Figure 15-21. *Office long shot 1*

Figure 15-22. *Office long shot 2*

Figure 15-23 shows another angle from inside the small office looking out to the larger one.

Figure 15-23. *Small office shot*

Figure 15-24 shows a long shot of the office hallway with all the lighting.

Figure 15-24. *Hallway long shot*

Finally, Figure 15-25 shows the reception area with the sofa and some foliage.

Figure 15-25. *Shot of the office reception area 1*

Another shot of the same place from a different angle is shown in Figure 15-26.

Figure 15-26. *Long shot of reception area 2*

Conclusion

You have now completed this book. I hope the information that you got from it has been useful. Creating a complete scene from scratch is a pretty big project, and it takes a lot of time and patience to finish.

Here are some additional useful tips for when you are working on a similar project.

- Gather references. References are very useful and important for creating anything. Have reference images for everything.

- Always name your assets properly. UE4 uses certain naming conventions to identify assets and their types, which is convenient when multiple people are working on the same project. SM_ is used for static meshes and followed by the asset name. M_ or MM_ is used for master materials. MI_ or _Inst is used for material instances. MF_ is used for material functions. BP_ is used for blueprint classes and objects. Use these as naming conventions for your assets.

- Create a plan/layout. Never go in blind. Create a rough layout for your level in software application like Photoshop. You can even hand-draw it.

- Start simple. Start with simple walls and floors to see whether your layout works or not. Blockout is important before going into detail.

- Layer details. When adding details, go in layer by layer. Start with a simple layout and then add larger details, such as furniture. After that, add smaller details, such as decorations.

- Always have a folder structure for storing your assets. When you start a new project, create the following folders immediately: Assets, Blueprints, and Maps. Inside the Assets folder, add Master_Materials, Material_Instances, Material_Functions, Meshes, and Textures. Inside Blueprints, add folders like Tools, Gameplay, and so forth. This allows you to handle and manage your assets well and organize your project.

Assets can be used in a variety of ways in your portfolio. In architectural visualization, there usually aren't restrictions on polygon count or performance because the scenes are entirely designed to show off your assets in the highest visual fidelity. In these cases, you can freely create whatever you want without worrying about light baking or polygons.

Of course, there are some restrictions. You shouldn't bring fully subdivided models into UE4 because it completely overloads the Engine. But if you have a decently powerful system, then UE4 can easily handle several hundred thousand polygons in a scene, depending on the complexity of the materials that you use.

It is best to optimize your assets because it allows your skills to be transferred to game development and VR, which has a strict memory budget. Make sure to keep your skills scalable.

These scenes can be easily used as a portfolio for Archviz scenes, but it is important to know Blueprints well to create more interactions. Blueprints is an entirely different subject that requires its own dedicated book.

Game-level design is a good environment to use as a portfolio to show off all of your skills. If planned well, you can create amazing scenes with a very small amount of tileable assets.

***

Index

A

Advanced Glass Material Pack, 289
Angle problem, 86–93
Architectural Visualization
   design application
      Blender, 12, 13
      3DS Max, 13
      Unity3D, 15
   Maya, design, 7
   Quixel Megascans, 10, 11, 167, 169–172
   Quixel Mixer, 9, 10
   substance painter, 8, 9
   UE4, 11, 12
Augmented reality (AR), 1

B, C

Blocking out, 22
   adding details, 49–58
   adding symmetry, 25–32
   angle problem, 86–93
   changing parameters, 22
   detailing phase, 78–86
   duplicate faces, 32–40
   extrude edges, 25
   flattening object, 23
   isolating inner object, 59–64, 66
   joining objects, 44–48
   making final adjustments, 69–77

multi-cut tool, 40–43
poly count, 96–101
remove unwanted faces, 67–69
scaling object, 23
Shader test, 93–96

D

Dirt
   active channel, 193
   add filter, 192
   alpha map slot, 197
   Blur filter, 192
   Blur intensity, 193
   controlling amount, 190
   disable all channels, 190, 191
   enabling symmetry, 199
   hard surfaces, 195, 196
   layer opacity, 194
   normal channel, 195
   normal map slot, 196
   normal painting, 197, 198
   painting details, 198
   paint layer, 194
   procedural effect, mesh, 191

E

Earpad result, 55
Edge Edit mode, 27, 28, 59, 65, 92

© Abhishek Kumar 2021
A. Kumar, *Immersive 3D Design Visualization*, https://doi.org/10.1007/978-1-4842-6597-0

M, N, O

P

Printed in the United States
By Bookmasters